Endorsements and Testimonials for
I Don't Wear A Suit
Victoria A. Seitz, Ph.D.

"Victoria Seitz is an expert in helping professionals look right for all business occasions—in *'I Don't Wear a Suit'* her guidance is contemporary, affordable, and appropriate for job seekers and senior leaders."

Virginia Moxley, Dean, College of Human Ecology, Kansas State University

"*'I Don't Wear A Suit'* is a must-have, must-read, must-keep-on-the-shelf book for young people just entering the work place as well as seasoned executives -- and don't forget those folks who wear jeans to work or Armani suits. Dr. Seitz takes her vast knowledge of fashion, trends and clothing do's and don'ts and applies them in an understandable format that is applicable in today's workplace. She transports us from the 20th to 21st century fashion etiquette and surprises the reader with what is and isn't acceptable clothing practices - giving the reader a level of 'dress sophistication' not common in today's world. *'I Don't Wear Suit'* should be looked upon as the The Amy Vanderbilt Complete *Book* of *Etiquette* for appropriate fashion practices."

Jay Vanier, CEO of CAFO'S BEST Waste Solutions LLC.

T0148146

"Victoria has done incredible research and provided an abundance of pertinent information in *'I Don't Wear A Suit,'* and it's spelled out in a way that folks will understand!"

Nancy Woolfolk, Designer

"Looking good IS very important! This is what I have learned from Dr. Seitz herself but also from her first book *Your Executive Image*. Sixteen years in the corporate world has taught me that good communication skills, hard work and your appearance all play key roles to your success. To this day I still refer to her book for myself and to those I mentor. We invest a lot into our education but it is equally important to invest in your appearance. I am thrilled that Dr. Seitz has written the new book *I Don't Where A Suit* because as she eludes to there is an ever changing environment in the workplace, casual does not equal a free for all. There is still a dress code out there and this book will help you understand that code, this book is a "must have" in your professional collection. Dress for success!!!!!"

Orlando Moreno, National Account Manager, Abbott Laboratories

"I've known Dr. Seitz for over 20 years. She is right on target with her advice. Anyone who is serious about moving up the company ladder or securing the perfect job needs to read and heed this book."

Martin Birnbach, President and CEO, MB&A Executive Search and Consulting

"Timeless, transforming and priceless! A powerful resource and a practical gift for yourself and others. Dr. Seitz unlocks the KEY to energizing your optimal success! Empower yourself and emerge with an updated image! Dr. Seitz is a trusted internationally known author and marketer. You will have greater opportunities with her leading-edge advice!"

Barbara Doebele Donovan, Target Marketing & Consulting

I Don't Wear A Suit!

A guide to style for ALL OF US

Victoria A. Seitz, Ph.D.

authorHOUSE®

AuthorHouse™
1663 Liberty Drive
Bloomington, IN 47403
www.authorhouse.com
Phone: 1-800-839-8640

First published by AuthorHouse 9/6/2011

ISBN: 978-1-4634-6831-6 (sc)
ISBN: 978-1-4634-6830-9 (e)

Library of Congress Control Number: 2011915037

Printed in the United States of America

Photography by Michael Schaffer.

Be the Best *You* can Be!

This book is dedicated to my father,
Lt. General Richard J. Seitz (retired),
An outstanding individual,
Who, without uttering a word, inspired greatness
In everyone he met.
Thanks so much, Dad!

Table of Contents

Acknowledgements

There are so many people to thank for making this idea come to fruition. First and foremost, I would like to thank my BFF Olesia Mihai, who allowed me to camp at her flat in Romania during my sabbatical to work on this project. It was a blast! Additionally, I'd like to thank my good friends in Iasi and Bucharest, Romania, who were so supportive such as Catia, Mirona, Mariana, Lulu and Ela. I also want to thank my stateside gal pals and friends who provided support, encouragement and love including Laura, Carol and Ed, Audrey, Shirley and Bob, Ruthie, Dennett, Purnima, and Jacque. In addition, I would like to thank my colleagues at California State University, San Bernardino who have been so supportive in all my endeavors. Special thanks go to my editor and coach Robin Quinn who really polished the manuscript and gave me great direction. I am also indebted to Barbara Donovan and Martin Birnbach for their keen insights into my proposal and manuscript – it's copyrighted and unisexed! Also special thanks go to Orlando Moreno, Nancy Woolfolk and Jay Vanier for their suggestions and support regarding the initial draft of the book. You truly made this book the best ever! Finally, I would like to thank my family, which has loved and supported me always – I am truly blessed and grateful! And to my dog, Pauly – you're the man! Life is measured by friendships; they give meaning to it all! Thank you!

Preface

It's still important to dress and look good for work. However, over the years, there has been a demise of professional dress – dressing for work has gotten downright sloppy. What's a company to do, let alone its employees? Meanwhile, there are all sorts of jobs and careers, and they necessitate appropriate dress for work, whether it's a law firm or a local factory.

It used to be that the only appropriate office attire that communicated success was the suit. Today, there is a continuum of options that are just as appropriate and successful-looking, depending on where you work and what you do. I don't wear a suit and I'm not about to buy one; yet I do make an effort to dress in a professional manner.

As a former fashion coordinator and retailer, and now a marketing educator, I can assure you that marketing yourself is just as important as having another business do this for you. Your image matters. It's no longer "Dress for Success" with just suits; nevertheless, what you wear has to communicate the best about you.

This book is the result of years of experience in fashion and marketing. Since my book, *Your Executive Image*, I have had the opportunity of working with hundreds of companies and individuals on dressing for the workplace, and I am now bringing that experience to you. This book is for men and women and with the information you will learn how to dress for your job and career. You'll be able to dress up or down, depending on what your needs are at the workplace. Today, there truly is a continuum of clothing possibilities that spell success, whether we work in a factory, argue a case in court, or teach.

You will learn the foundations of good style and design, and you'll be able to use color to develop your own individual look that works for you. You'll know how to create impact with accessories, and you will develop the skill of maximizing your assets and minimizing your liabilities for a look that's coordinated and appealing. I have also included information to help you take care of your clothing investment, whether it's cleaning the clothes or removing stains. As well, I have provided background to help business owners and human resource professionals develop dress policies that will aid in providing a positive work environment and a consistent image for the brand. Finally, to help clarify the terms used in this book and in the industry a glossary is provided for you.

With this purchase, you have acquired the handbook for dressing great in today's workplace. You now have the tools to look your best and successful no matter what you do.

Happy reading!

Introduction

It's a New World Out There!

In just the past five years, the world of work has changed as well as the clothing we wear for it! What was once considered "Business Casual" is simply business as usual. The high-tech industry, according to Google, Apple and Facebook, has transformed the image of what an executive looks like or what anyone wears to work. In the past, business attire was a suit; however, that no longer represents all professionals or the average work environment.

In my former book, *Your Executive Image*, the suit was the principal form of nonverbal communication for the workplace. When I was promoting it back in the early 90s, some people would say, ". . . but I don't wear a suit!" And that's true, particularly now. Today, there are a lot of jobs and careers that don't require a suit but the need to look professional is paramount. Moreover, in many occupations, going to work without a jacket, in jeans, or wearing other formerly "casual" clothing is now considered appropriate. When I look through the pages of catalogs from which I once purchased suits, these items are no longer part of the retailer's merchandise mix. Things have indeed changed, but neither for better or worse.

Bottom line: Realize that dressing for work is just that, dressing appropriately. Coming to work looking like Hollywood's latest red carpet fashion stroll, the cover of GQ, or the sexy housewives of Orange County doesn't work for business either. These are not definitions of business attire. Work apparel is still conservative, since building a bridge and functioning easily with different people on a daily basis is a must. We just have more options than formal or informal or suits and business casual.

Why the Change?

Among the reasons that the suit has not remained the prevailing code of dress for the workplace is *economics*. The cost of living has risen and buying a suit can be very expensive. The last global recession really impacted individuals' ability to maintain a roof over their heads and food for their family. Employers have become sensitive to this issue and have relaxed their dress policies to accommodate this new reality.

Another reason is the *diversity* in the workplace. We are fortunate to have a multitude of ethnicities living in the US as well as throughout the world. And in this environment, each person brings their own style of dress to the workplace – whether for religious or other cultural reasons. In addition to that is the *influence of pop culture*. Actors, designers, singers and artists of all types are bringing their own take on what constitutes dressing up for events such as TV interviews or even the Oscars!

Another reason why the suit is not the mainstay for work is the *influence of women* in the workplace. Women have long established themselves at work, and wearing a navy or black suit that mimics menswear is not advantageous for them today. Amazing, but it only took a court case for women to be allowed to wear pants to work!

Additionally, *baby boomers*, who make up the largest market segment globally, are aging, and with that comes the need for more comfortable clothing suitable for work. The members of this segment have established themselves in their profession and they can now take it a little bit easier. Lycra-blended fabrics, softer materials, and less structured apparel with more ease have replaced structure and confinement found in traditional work apparel. The baby boomers were the generation that vowed to always wear jeans, and so, with the introduction of a fine denim weave suitable for trousers, we now have the ability to go back to wearing our "jeans" even to work!

Finally, there is the *influence of business casual* policies, once initiated to boost employee morale and confined to "Casual Fridays." This look has now become the mode for every day of the week. As a result, the clothing industry has created lots of options that are considered just as appropriate for work.

No Longer "One Size Fits All"

What you wear to work makes all the difference for you, your workplace, and ultimately your business success. First of all, when you feel good about how you look, you feel better about yourself. At work, you take on a business-like, serious attitude, and with it, you perform better. When you look good, people around you respond in a positive manner. When you take the time to dress appropriately for work, coworkers and customers respond to you as a professional.

In the past, there was just one "uniform," the suit, that defined a professional. Now there are many that are just as appropriate and "business like." Earlier, it almost seemed that if you wore a suit then you were "dressed for success." However, you can now be in jeans and be seen just as serious about your work and success. We have dropped the "one size fits all" model of what constitutes work apparel or a successful business image, and this has opened the door to many more acceptable options.

Yes, today you have many choices available besides the suit, depending on your corporate culture, where you live, and what you do. In fact, what we wear to work is a continuum of possibilities that may change, depending on the various needs of your business, the seasons of the year, and who you're meeting. It is no longer an "either or" situation; it's a range of choices for the workplace that work for you and works for business.

Enjoy!

Looking Good IS Important

We are a very visual society! With YouTube and the variety of entertainment shows, gossip magazines as well as the hundreds of reality programs, we give a lot of clout to what we see. As someone in the advertising and marketing industry, I'd say that exposure on television is where it's at. With over 500 channels we have a lot to watch! Today, trends and fads get the majority of their forward motion via the media either through TV or the Internet, both being visual in nature. And because of this influence, media personalities and marketers use clothing to impact the audience in a positive manner. For you, the influence you have with others is also enhanced through the visual signals you emit. This is referred to as *Attribution Theory*.

Attribution Theory

Human beings subconsciously (or perhaps unconsciously) size up other people, places and things during first encounters based on very little information. *Attribution Theory* states that for human beings to function in a society where we face a barrage of stimuli constantly, we need to be able to categorize it quickly and do so on limited information. It's kind of like organizing your computer files, putting all the files in various folders as well as the recycle bin. Or think about all the emails you receive – some you read, some you delete, and some you save for later. That's how we, as human beings, can simplify our lives and move on.

So understanding this mental process, what are the nonverbal messages or cues that human beings use to categorize people who they encounter on a daily basis? Some of these factors include the clothes worn, mannerisms, body image, and overall appearance. Everything about a person communicates messages about them. For example, if you see someone and they have acne, you might infer that they're young, maybe a teenager. If we see someone with glasses, perhaps we might infer that they're smart (or want to be) or do a lot of reading. If we see a woman covering her head in a certain way, we may infer that she is a member of a particular religion or from another culture. Again, we make inferences about people on very little information, and this subsequently influences how we interact with them.

This is why so much consideration is given to appearance. The sum of the factors – such as clothing, body language, mannerisms, hair and body type, which constitute a person's appearance and together may be considered beautiful and favorable in the eye of the beholder – subsequently promotes interaction between individuals. In fact, appearance is about 55 percent of the evaluation in first impression situations. Frankly, in the first 3-4 seconds, people size up those they meet on all the cues that are available. All of this is done before we ever say hello! And once that happens, we also assess whether what they say fulfills those expectations or breaks them. As they say, first impressions count and are so critical in the workplace, in interviews, and on first dates!

Further, in 30 seconds, people make at least 11 assumptions about you – including your occupation, social status, marital status, trustworthiness, credibility, ancestry and (most important) your likelihood to succeed! Everyone wants to be around a winner! In job interviews, about 75 percent of the decision to hire you is based on your appearance. The actual interview itself is about whether you fulfill the expectations set when you both first saw each other. Additionally, there is an 8 to 20 percent difference in the entry salary you receive based on your appearance. Maybe you look like a person that the company wants to invest in and maybe you don't – it's up to you!

All across the world, there are distinct definitions of what is beautiful. What is beautiful in one country may be perceived as ugly in the next. Why is beauty so important? It seems that most people associate with *what is beautiful with what is good.* There has been a lot of research on this topic with these same findings. For example, a study done in measuring student success found that students who were perceived as "beautiful" were also perceived to be smarter and more inclined to succeed in school. Outward beauty is defined by a culture and it drives companies to offer many products and services to enhance it.

Moreover, research has shown that people are attracted to others that *dress like them*. Often, someone's appearance infers their political beliefs, values and attitudes. Let's say you are interviewing for a position at Saks Fifth Avenue. Do you look like a Saks Fifth Avenue employee or someone from Walmart? You decide – do you want to look the part?

Further Considerations

It's important to realize that impressions can be broken. For example, if we have little experience working with persons with disabilities, we may hold negative impressions based on individuals' outward physical disabilities. Yet when we get to know disabled people, we could find that they are brilliant and wonderful to work with. Or maybe you meet someone and extend a hand, and they take it, but they give you a very weak handshake. This may be due to problems with arthritis, but you might assume they are a meek person. Or perhaps you're trying to do business with someone from another country, say Japan. You're frustrated because they don't give you eye contact. Well, in many Asian countries, eye contact is perceived as inappropriate and where they do look might be your forehead. As with first impressions, nothing is in stone; however, we want to put our best foot forward.

When we get to know someone, appearance becomes less important as the relationship flourishes. Think about the dating scene. For a while, you will look your best for each encounter. Then, over time, both of you will begin to relax your ways as other aspects of the relationship become more important. It's almost as if appearance sets the stage for a potential relationship.

This "relaxing with time" also applies to the business setting; however, there is an important difference. Although we may work with our officemates day in and day out, a business usually has new clients or customers entering the picture on a regular basis. Given this, your appearance remains critical to the business's continued success, and this is why many firms have dress policies.

Role Theory

Another theory that operates successfully in the workplace is *Role Theory*. Basically, the theory states is that when we see someone in a uniform – perhaps in a military uniform – we will conduct ourselves in a manner respectful of it. In addition, the person wearing the uniform will usually take on the role associated with it, such as a military officer. Often, companies will have its employees wear a uniform in part because of this theory. Also, this policy helps the company maintain their brand image and saves employees money on their clothing budget! Many companies, such as hospitals, airlines, and restaurants, have addressed the issue of appearance by mandating uniforms.

Role Theory also relates to how we dress for work outside the realm of a uniform. Many companies that introduced a casual dress code found that they had to revoke the privilege because employees took it too far. Not only did it sabotage the company's brand image but the change affected employee performance, too. Generally, when there is a lack of consideration regarding our dress for work, there is also a lack of professionalism in performance in our work. It impacts the quality of our interactions with our peers, customers and coworkers as well.

Although you may dislike the employee dress policy at your workplace, think about this. Inasmuch as you are trying to reinforce YOUR brand image through your appearance and mannerism so is a business. A brand's image is critical to a company's success. We buy BRANDS of products and services based on the image or the meaning of the brand to us. Therefore, businesses try to control all aspects of their brand, including the contact points that involve employees. If the brand name is important to you, then you can understand why companies try to manage their brand all the way down to their employees. If bank employees wore their favorite jeans, would you really think they know what they're doing in trying to execute your house loan? There is a reason businesses want us to dress for work.

Being Your Best

We're all individuals and it's important to communicate that. Yet, when working and dealing with people who come from different backgrounds and experiences, we go beyond our peer group and need to keep this in mind when getting dressed. Most of us recognize the value of individuality and therefore the definition of what is appropriate for work is rather open; however, we don't want to totally ignore the significance of the clothes we choose.

Many of us are established in our profession and perhaps have a reputation. It's important to maintain that positive reputation in all associations, either with clients, prospects, employers, coworkers and employees. Looking your best shows respect for others and makes you feel good. Think about it … if you show up in your sweats to a business meeting, what would that communicate to prospective clients, customers, employees or coworkers? You may be an expert in your field; however, it's still important to connect with others and communicate your expertise instantly.

Looking good, appearing professional, and communicating your individuality is possible without being a fashion expert. When I was a fashion coordinator at Burdines, now Macy's, the navy blue suit was it for work; however, things have changed dramatically. We are not relegated to a prescription regarding what to wear. Moreover, developing your own style is paramount in business because it communicates your leadership ability and your capacity to take risks.

By using the guidelines presented in this book, you can develop that look that says you and only you. The right look will also build a bridge with those you deal with in your business. In the chapters that follow, we'll cover options for you to be the best you can be in this new business environment. Since men and women have different needs, we will address those separately so you can focus on the areas of concern to you.

Have fun!

2

The New Continuum of Dressing for Success

The workplace has become a kinder, gentler place regarding what to wear. However, as mentioned earlier, that does not mean that dress is not important. Your level of professionalism, expertise, and likelihood to succeed is communicated first and foremost in your appearance, with a large part of this being made up by what you select to wear. The fact that "suits" are not required for a lot of businesses does not equate with tattered jeans and a T-shirt. The clothes we saw in workplace scenes in the movie, *The Social Network,* are not business as usual; instead, work apparel is different than clothing worn for socializing with your friends.

So the more relaxed atmosphere of work and the many wardrobe options available to us are often givens. Based on this truth, here is a new approach that will help guide you on what exactly should constitute your work wardrobe. Today's formula presents a continuum of possibilities based on the culture of the business, where you are based, and your profession/occupation. For instance, wearing a suit in my Southern California town is not very common; people are just more casual here. Perhaps your company's culture is also more relaxed rather than traditional, so a suit may not be necessary.

However, whether you are a man or woman, note that the suit (matching jacket and bottom) is NOT dead and it is appropriate in select situations and fields such as law. Still, in many instances, having the option of wearing a jacket or a blazer will elicit the same professionalism and not be deemed too formal for your business environment such as teaching or marketing. Finally, as an individual established in your career or in high-tech organizations, there are avenues for dressing which are considered appropriate for work that don't mandate a suit or a jacket and jeans are ok. Yet, realize that when it comes to a job interview, most times a suit (including a tie for men) is the best option.

I have broken down this continuum of work apparel into three distinct categories, and in this chapter, I will describe each and how they function. The categories are:

1. Suits required
2. Jackets optional
3. Jeans permitted

You say, JEANS?! Yes, in many businesses, jeans are OK. Further, given that denim has come a long way regarding fabrication, denim trousers are quite acceptable when jackets are optional. The dress continuum ranges from very traditional to very relaxed contemporary business attire. However, no matter what your profession or job might be, dressing for work each morning requires some thought as to the appropriate look for day ahead. Let's investigate this further.

Suits Required

This category is the most formal of the three categories along the continuum. In these cases, a suit is required at the workplace and usually for men a tie may be expected as well. Some professions – such as law, banking and finance – would more than likely require a suit, as well as a corporate culture that is more traditional and formal. Furthermore, where you live has an impact, too. When living in a major metropolitan city, such as New York or London, your workplace would be more inclined to require suits.

A suit communicates a formal and professional appearance with a matching top and bottom. When suits are required though there can be other options that are just as appropriate – such as blazers for men. For women, there are blazers, as well as short and long jackets, that can be worn with a skirt, pants or over a dress. Let's consider the options for men and then for women. Bottom line is when suits are required the mainstay of your wardrobe will be suits.

For Men: If the workplace requires a suit, consider building your wardrobe around a single suit and then adding blazers that coordinate

– particularly if you're just getting started. For example, beginning with a grey suit, you can add a navy blazer and a camel sport coat. A navy blazer can be paired with khaki, olive, camel, taupe or light gray slacks, plus jeans for your casual time. Now you have access to a multitude of blazers to choose from to build your wardrobe without investing in suits all the time. There are blazers in raw silk and in linen, besides the basic wool. Plus, there are a wide variety of easy-care fabrics such as Tencel and polyester blends that are also suitable.

The suit and tie is the ultimate in formal business attire, and it communicates instant expertise. Further, a suit and tie often is expected by those in certain industries as well as by the clients they serve.

When it comes to this category, conservative is best. Focus on established fabrics and patterns, such as tweed, herringbone, gabardines in solids and subtle patterns such as pin and chalk stripes. Glenn plaids rather than scotch plaids are better when the business mandates a suit because it's expected and established in business. However, building from your selection of suits you might even consider getting a black blazer, either in a double- or single-breasted style, since black is considered a neutral, and it therefore goes with a lot in your wardrobe.

Choose established silhouettes regarding suits, sport coats and blazers such as American and European cuts. For this category, being a fashionista is not the focus. Jackets in bulky fabrics, novelty colors and textures and with a lot of designs are not appropriate. You'll want the jacket to land below your derriere and to fit correctly. Choose a blazer or coat that is lined and offers a traditional fit, including set-in sleeves and tailored-notched collar lapels. A single-breasted jacket can have two to three buttons and the width of the lapels may vary depending on current fashion trends. Accessories for this category include kerchiefs in the breast pocket, leather belts, and shoes, as well as subtle pattern hosiery. Jewelry should be kept to a minimum.

For Women: Given that this category requires the most formal of business attire, women still have a lot of options. A suit is probably something that you will want several of; however, it is not the only alternative. Consider a dress, either with or without sleeves, and a matching or contrasting jacket. And like men, a great addition to your wardrobe that helps build variety are blazers in black, navy, gray, taupe, camel and/or olive. You can team a navy blazer with jeans for your casual time or with a pair of slacks for work. Depending on fashion trends, blazers fall below the waist and can land mid to below the derriere.

Traditional suit jackets and blazers, either with or without lapels, should be structured or lined to provide stability to the fabric. Such features also make it easier to put these on over dresses and shirts. Details might include single or double welt pockets, breast pockets, patch or slit pockets. Plus there may or may not be a vent in the back. Regarding princess seams, let them provide a pleasing shape to the overall silhouette; still, you don't want the jacket to be so fitted that you can't really move comfortably. Tailored and polished is what you're aiming for.

Another style of jacket for consideration is the box-style, also known as Chanel-style. With or without a lapel or collar and less tailored than a blazer, this style is great because it works for a multitude of body types. If you're like me, a pear, the box style adds more "weight" to the upper torso and balances the shape. This style of jacket can be teamed with pants, skirts or dresses to create a pleasing suit-like ensemble appropriate for a formal business environment.

The types of fabrics to consider for suits include gabardine, polyester blends, tweed, wool, Tencel, linen blend, cotton, raw silk and some of the newer synthetics. Consider solid colors or subtle patterns such as Glenn plaid, pin- or chalk-striped, and herringbone so as to give yourself options for coordinating it with other pieces of your wardrobe. Like for men, businesses that require suits for women are seeking the ultimate in formal business attire; in these cases, conservative is best when it comes to choices.

Accessories work to pull your look together, and they include scarves, belts and jewelry, such as lapel pins and earrings. Hosiery and shoes are essential details that warrant a conservative professional appeal, and these might include pumps and slip-ons. Stay away from flats, athletic shoes and sandals.

Jackets Optional

For such businesses as marketing, fashion, sales, education, real estate and a multitude of others, jackets are optional. Here you have the option of wear a jacket or not and will be perfectly dressed for the office. As opposed to having to wear a suit where a top such as jacket or blazer and a matching or coordinating bottom is necessary, when jackets are optional just wearing slacks and a shirt for men or skirt and blouse or women is deemed suitable for business. Having jackets optional for many companies signaled business casual in the past; however, for many, this form of workplace attire communicates an approachable professionalism, and it does not put off customers. Further, if you're in sales, one day may take you to someone's office inside a building where a jacket is preferable, while the next day you could be outside at a construction site. Often you want to appear professional but also appropriate for where you're at.

If you're a man, you may be required to wear a tie but a jacket is your choice. Sometimes you may choose to wear a jacket but not a tie since it's not required. If you live in Phoenix in the summer, jackets are definitely not worn even in retail. It's too darn hot!

In this category, we have the opportunity to relax our look with greater leeway when it comes to introducing fashion and our own personal style into our professional appearance. Further, nontraditional fabrics, such as fine denim twills and knits, and those with interesting textures can be considered. However, let me caution you, satins, loose knits such as netting, brocade, shiny metallics, and sheer fabrics are a "no go" for work. You might consider leather or suede for your jackets but stay away from the leather pants unless you're in the fashion business.

For Men: Although jackets are optional, great consideration must be made in your choice of pants, shirts and such accessories as belts, shoes and socks. Depending on the type of business, you may even consider a tailored denim blazer if you want to wear one. Blazers and sport coats (either structured or unstructured), worn with shirts and trousers, provide an approachable yet professional appearance. In this category, V-neck and crew neck sweaters and cardigans are another option to create versatility in your wardrobe, and provide warmth during the winter. Vests give men another option outside of a jacket. If you choose to wear a jacket, single- or double- breasted blazers are great choices. When you're trying to find these items in a store, keep in mind that they are considered suit separates or sportswear.

Regarding tops, shirts (either short or long sleeved), turtlenecks, polos, or pullover sweaters are options. When it comes to sleeves for dress shirts, consider long-sleeved varieties. Even when temperatures are hot, it looks nicer to roll up the cuff a couple times rather than wearing a short-sleeved shirt. For button-down sport shirts short is fine. However, when it comes to whether you should wear your shirt tucked in or out, tucked in with a belt is best. Even though the overall look of this second category is not as traditional as when a suit is required, your professional appearance is a must.

When it comes to pants, dress pants, either plain front or pleated, in fabrics such as cotton twill or wool blends, with or without a cuff are great choices. Your pants should be in excellent condition without holes or fraying on the edges. Regarding the color and design of the belt, go towards a conservative belt buckle and the shoes and belts should match in color. Shoes might include loafer styles with flaps and tassels. If you desire comfort, there are many companies that offer softer soles and leather uppers that enhance comfort for everyday wear. Avoid the athletic shoes, flip flops and sandals.

For Women: Options, options, options ... but still professional appearance counts! Again, like men, you can choose to wear a jacket or not; however, there are lots of possibilities. For example, consider tunic tops with pants and a short jacket for interest. Fashion becomes a player in this category, particularly if you're in the creative fields such as interior and fashion design, architecture and theater arts. If you want to go sleeveless, however, do wear a jacket or perhaps a knit cardigan. Skirts in a variety of lengths (yet a minimum of three inches above the knee and a maximum mid-calf) are choices to consider. Pants also have a multitude of lengths; everything from city shorts (which are about three inches above the knee) to cropped, ankle and regular lengths work well. Try fitted shirts worn alone with pants or a skirt.

Dresses such as a sheath or shift with princess seams worn with a belted cardigan work well for this category. Consider two-piece dressing that can mix and match with pieces already in your wardrobe, and also sweater sets, pull-over sweaters, and bulky turtlenecks as options for colder months.

Fabrics might include traditional ones, as mentioned above, or those with interesting designs and textures. Stay away from metallic, brocade, translucent and sheer-type fabrics. Although this category allows a lot of freedom of expression, your appearance must remain professional. Denim trousers and jackets that are tailored are an option but DO NOT wear jeans (there is a difference!). Accessories, such as scarves, hosiery and jewelry, play an even more important role within this category in personalizing your style. Shoes such as pumps, tailored boots, open-toed shoes (not sandals), slip-ons and loafers are options for the category.

Jeans Permitted

Yes, there are some occupations where jeans, nice jeans, are an option for work. Nice jeans do not have holes or a lot of stitching (which has seen its day in fashion). Additionally, this category might include uniforms found in many occupations. It is imperative that anything that you wear for work is clean, pressed, without tears and lost buttons, and fits properly. Often at this stage, most people don't give much consideration to what they're wearing or how they are wearing it. They assume that anything goes, but that is farthest from the truth. Communicating your professionalism is just as important within the "Jeans Permitted" category. In many high-tech companies, such as Apple or Facebook, jeans and T-shirts are commonplace, and it's OK just as long as they're in good condition for work – there is a difference!

Pants and skirts in denim and a variety of casual fabrics are the highlight of this category. Some jobs that might fall under the "Jeans Permitted" category, depending on the corporate culture, might include retail, restaurant, music, and those in the film industry where being able to move equipment and work a scene is a must. This category does NOT exclude other dress options suggested above, but permits denim. Hence, consider hard-working fabrics such as twill found in Docker brand pants, as well as some fashion alternatives such as longer skirts.

For Men: As mentioned earlier, jeans and T-shirts are acceptable in many types of occupations; however, if considering them, have a good pair of jeans and several work T-shirts without writing or graphics on them unless the shirt has a company identification on it. Jeans need to land at the natural waist and have either a straight or boot-cut leg (slightly flared leg), and T-shirts need to be in really good condition and substantial enough in weight that they have body and don't show through. Regarding the style of the T-shirt, try one with short or long sleeves as opposed to sleeveless tanks. Consider cargo pants but avoid camouflage or military-type apparel. If shorts are ok choose Bermuda length in good condition. Consider leather jackets and vests for variety and long-sleeved flannel, denim or suede shirts. Hawaiian shirts are great if you live in Hawaii or California but be sure that they are not loud and overwhelming with neon-colored designs. Regarding shoes, consider those devoted to comfort, such as athletic shoes; but again, refrain from loud, highly detailed ones that draw attention to your feet rather than to your face. As well, avoid flip-flops and sandals.

Choose pants that have a classic look with minimum detail. If you wear a shirt with a hem, you'll want to tuck it in and wear a belt with a conservative belt buckle. Avoid belt buckles that are large and ornate and save those for your personal time. Light jackets are great; however, avoid "hoodies" and hats of any kind. As well, avoid sweatpants, warm-up suits and other athletic apparel, since you're going to work, not playing baseball. Consider bringing your gym bag with such clothes in it if that will be a part of your day.

If you wear a uniform, it should fit and be clean and pressed. If you need to provide your own shoes, make sure they are made for comfort and coordinate in color with the uniform. As well, jewelry should to be kept to a minimum.

For Women: It is just as important to dress professionally at this end of the continuum as it is with more formal traditional businesses. Seek tailored styles and avoid sexy, revealing clothing, such as skirts with slits in the front and side. Exposed midriffs and cleavage are also not appropriate, as well as wearing fashion's latest craze. As mentioned previously, what you wear to work needs to be clean, pressed, coordinated, accessorized and it needs to fit. Consider polo, crew- and V-neck style shirts but avoid halter tops. If you wear jeans, consider straight legged or boot-cut styles with minimal detailing. The jeans should land at your natural waist or slightly below.

Consider unstructured jackets, such as jean jackets, and cargo pants with limited detailing; however, avoid "hoodies" and hats. Pants and skirts need to land at the natural waist or a little below but avoid hip-hugger styles. As well, skirts, shorts and dresses should be no shorter than three inches above the knee.

Save the sun dresses, halter styles, as well as beach cover-ups for your personal time. As well, avoid sweat pants and work-out apparel, even warm-up suits for the office. Consider cargo pants but avoid camouflage, military-type apparel. As well, introduce various types of skirts – split skirts, mid-calf length types, gathered, pleated or plain front – in denim, leather or suede, with boots or tailored flats for your office attire. Avoid leggings, jeggings (leggings out of denim), flip-flops and very high platform shoes – *period!* Greek-styled, gladiator sandals that go up the leg need to be worn during your personal time and not for work. If you want to wear athletic shoes, consider those that have minimum detail and non-bright colors. Have a pair for work and one for your time away from work.

If you wear a uniform, make sure that it's clean and pressed and fits you. If you need to provide your own shoes, seek those that are comfortable and tailored. Choose a color for the shoes which compliments your uniform. Jewelry is best kept at a minimum, and if you wear hose, consider tights but avoid fishnets.

Conclusion

If your company does NOT have a dress policy, look at what your supervisor or the owner is wearing for clues. Also, use the three categories mentioned above to help guide yourself regarding what works for work and you. More details regarding options for each will be spelled out in the next chapter.

Bottom line: Realize that your appearance counts at work, no matter what job you have!

3

Workplace Dress 101: Getting Started

When someone is concerned about the best way to present themselves for work, they can worry that this means changing everything in their closet and buying a new wardrobe. However, that's not the case. When it comes to looking appropriate for any type of job or profession, there are some basics that apply to all. You don't have to buy a whole new wardrobe or become someone else. Yet given that you're communicating your expertise and professionalism in an instant, there are some things that must be addressed. Many of these things you may do already – if so, great! For others, these are the basics that will take you to the next level in building your work wardrobe.

Let's get started.

Organize

First of all, you'll want to go in your closet and organize it. How can you build your work wardrobe if you don't know what you have in it? By organizing your closet, you'll be able to find the key pieces that will jumpstart your "look" for work and minimize large purchases. Once you're organized, you'll be able to build your wardrobe off the key colors that communicate your individual taste while being appropriate for the workplace.

If you have hangers that are supposed to hang one item but have several, let's say shirts, on them, that's a clue that some things need to go. Here are some pointers for deciding what to let go:

- If you haven't worn it in a year, turn it loose.
- If you're a size or two too big or small for it, take it out.

- If it reminds you of the last Janis Joplin concert you went to in the 70s, get rid of it.
- If you don't like it, let it go.

Put a pile together and give a nice tax-deductible donation to Goodwill, the Salvation Army, your favorite charity (such as "Dress for Success," www.dressforsuccess.org), a domestic violence or homeless shelter, or a local school or university. That way, you'll be helping many people with things that are still good but you don't wear.

Now move things around and put your pants together, shirts together, dresses together and so forth. Organize them by color from light to dark. If you have a lot of room or if you have two closets for your clothes, you might want to have one just for work and one for outside work. Depending on what you do for a living, you may find that the two differ extensively while others find their work and personal time outfits are interchangeable. This depends on your profession, work culture and where you live.

To help keep your clothes in shape, you may consider plastic or wooden hangers rather than metal ones that can rust and stain your clothes. If you have knits, consider padded hangers and/or shelving to keep them from losing their shape. Regarding shoes, consider keeping them in see-through plastic shoe boxes. That's what I do and it keeps the dust off of them.

Build a Wardrobe Around Neutrals

Once you've organized your closet, you'll see the colors you're most attracted to among the clothes. Given that, what are the colors that you could integrate into your main pieces, such as jackets, skirts and pants, which will coordinate with everything you have? There are neutrals that allow you to wear your favorite colors and look coordinated. The neutrals for work include:

- Olive
- Taupe, camel, khaki and beige
- Dark chocolate
- Black
- Navy
- Gray

Wear your favorite colors in a shirt or blouse with a skirt, trousers or jacket that is a neutral. It really makes it easy to dress in the morning, if you're like me. I can barely see early in the day given that it's often still dark when I'm dressing for work and need to have everything coordinated with one another.

Stick to Classics

As someone who worked in the "fashion" business and is currently in marketing, I know how to get you to buy five times a year – it's called fashion. Fashion is an accepted manner of doing something or a style accepted by a group of people for a specific period of time. If you focus your wardrobe on *classic styles*, you will not look dated. Some examples include trench coats, coat dresses, navy blazers, shifts, sport coats, Chanel jackets, denim shirts, turtlenecks and polo tops, button-down collar shirts, wing-tip shoes, and even five-pocket jeans are seen year in and year out throughout the fashion magazines. They might be shown in a different fabric or variation of the silhouette but it is still a classic.

There are classic fabric patterns as well that include but are not limited to glen plaids, regimental stripe, hounds-tooth, herringbone, pin-striped, chalk-striped, tartan plaids, madras and Scotch plaids to name a few. You may say, "Ho-hum ... how boring" but often we translate someone wearing classic apparel as being affluent. When you consider some of our top designers who have been around forever, such as Ralph Lauren, Calvin Klein, Georgio Armani, Oscar de la Renta and Coco Chanel, you see that their inspiration has been interpreted into classic wearable styles that have lasted for years. If you want to update your wardrobe, oftentimes that can be done successfully through accessories or through a key piece such as a white shirt. With classics, you'll always be in fashion.

Buy for Investment

We have to watch our nickels no matter how much or how little we make. However, when I say this, I am not even suggesting buying the most expensive. Years in the clothing and marketing industries have taught me that designer apparel has perhaps some of your highest markups when it comes to retail prices. That's because we expect the price to be higher than other clothing and we are willing to pay for it. As well, for anything that is in demand, the markup will be high resulting in a high retail price. In fact, I recently read that the average markup for denim jeans was 1,000 percent. Well, yeah, it's everywhere and people want it. Jeans, a 1,000 percent markup, what am I really paying for?

Bottom line: When it comes to buying clothing, allocate the majority of that finite budget to your work clothes. Further, when it comes to quality, you'll want the better quality items closest to your face. More detail on what makes quality apparel in Chapter 13. However, realize that just because a piece of clothing is expensive doesn't mean that it's better. You can find quality at any price; you just have to know what to look for.

Choose Great Fabrics

This can be hard to do if you live in Phoenix but there are some fabrics that work from winter to spring. Further, there are a multitude of synthetics that are comfortable in all types of climates. One of the best fabrics all round is wool in a tropical weight. Wool keeps you warm in the winter and cool and dry in the summer. I can get into all that textile jargon; however, it depends on the finest of the yarn and the weave. If you're looking for easy care fabrics, the natural fibers blended with synthetics such as linen-polyester blends are wonderful. Wool and polyester as well as cotton and polyester maintain the wonderful properties of the natural fibers while giving you the ease of care found in synthetics.

Today, a lot of fabrics are blended with Lycra which allows the fabric to give a bit for comfort. Comfort IS important and textile manufacturers are creating fabrics that are comfortable, soft and professional for work. All sorts of fabrics, such as wool, cotton, rayon and silk, are being blended with Lycra spandex to provide ease of movement without sacrificing a polished appearance. Knits, another option, are a mainstay for any work wardrobe in zip-up cardigans, tops, dresses, skirts and pants. Understand fabric properties to find the best combination that works for where you live and what you do.

If you travel extensively, you may want to incorporate more knits and synthetics into your professional wardrobe. If you work in a humid and hot climate, such as Hong Kong or Singapore, lightweight cottons work best. If your work takes you to cold as well as warm climates, you might consider tropical-weight wool blends in key pieces that will take you anywhere.

Accessorize for Impact

No matter what you do, where you live, who you are or what your corporate culture is, you will be incorporating accessories into your wardrobe. Frankly, they are the key pieces that pull an ensemble together and can update your look for very little money. Men and women both have a wide variety of accessories that are the key to creating impact and communicating your individuality.

For men, examples include pocket squares, ties, belts, man bags, socks, shoes, scarves, shirts and jewelry – just to name a few. For women, they include jewelry, handbags, scarves, hosiery and belts. For either gender, going overboard on accessorizing an outfit can lead to confusion; however, every ensemble needs some accessories to complete the look. The role of accessories is to lead the eye to your best asset, your face, so consider this when adding scarves, belts and jewelry. Shoes and hosiery need to compliment rather than be the star. For example, hosiery should either match the color of the shoe or pants/skirts. Men, dark socks are preferred over white for work, so have them closely match your shoes or your pants. Patterns are great for socks; however, again, you don't want to draw the eye downward.

Since the movie *Disclosure*, there has been a question as to the necessity of hosiery at work. Demi Moore looked great in this office thriller without hose and established a precedent regarding sheers at the workplace. However, it's up to you. In the summer, perhaps not, but make sure your legs are cleanly shaven. Sheer hosiery really makes your legs look good and hides the bruises and broken veins. As well, hosiery is a great accessory. Also, if you have tired legs or need extra help, support hose, available for men and women, will make it easier to last throughout the day. Particularly if you work in retail, support hose are a must.

When it comes to jewelry for men, the question of earrings comes up. Should you or shouldn't you? If you're in the creative fields, earrings are well accepted; however, figure out the corporate culture and whether you're dealing with a conservative audience. If you're in sales and meeting new clients, it might be better to start conservative and then introduce earrings later. Consider something small and discreet. As for women, if you're in the creative fields, then deck the halls; however, in more formal environments, gold, silver or pearls create the air of affluence. More information about jewelry and other key accessories can be found in Chapter 10.

Makeup Is Optional, Skincare Is Essential

In this age where youth is glorified, having skin that is dry and wrinkled will really add years to your perceived age. It is so tough to be an older worker these days and I mean someone in their 40s, 50s, 60s and 70s. So it's essential, whether you're a man or woman, that you take care of your skin. Both genders have equal footing when it comes to skin care products; it's just a matter of getting in the routine of using them and the right ones. One product is, for sure, sun block – not sunscreen. Skin cancer is on the rise, so avoid tanning salons and tanning at the lake, beach or river. Yes, I know a tan makes you look good and perhaps feel good, too; however, the sun damage that results will age you dramatically! Consider bronzers for the tanned look without the damage.

Get in the habit of cleansing, toning and moisturizing your skin. After a shower or bath, put lotion on your body to keep it supple as well. Especially in the winter months, moisturizing after bathing minimizes the itchy discomfort experienced at this time. Even during the summer, put on a moisturizer after bathing. For your face, a non-soap cleanser is what you want. If you don't know your skin type, seek professional help from an aesthetician.

For women, when it comes to makeup, I have a simple message: don't prep for the night. Heavy makeup is not appropriate, no matter what you do for a living. A tinted moisturizer, some blush, lip gloss and perhaps some mascara is about all a woman needs. The key to foundation is to blend it on your face and past the chin line. As well, make sure you have plenty of light when you're putting it on – this will avoid adding too much. If you want to add some eye shadow, choose subtle tones such as olive, navy, deep purples, smoky browns blended across the eyelid. Don't experiment with loud colors like turquoise, pink and yellow at work. If you have blond lashes and light brows, use brown mascara. If you have darker features and complexion, black is perfect.

As we age, our once long lashes cease to exist and our brows lose their fullness. Eyebrows frame the eyes so consider filling them in with a brow pencil (ash blonde is great for light or dark brows as a pencil color) or get them colored. If you have lost much of your brows consider getting them tattooed; however, get professional help to do this. Likewise, permanent cosmetics are an option if you don't like putting your makeup on daily.

Men's makeup includes tinted moisturizer, bronzer and eyelash/brow gels and more. If you find that these products would be helpful, get professional advice first regarding their use and benefits. For more information regarding caring for your skin go to Chapter 12.

Mix Up Fabric Patterns

Today, we like a lot of stimulation. Solids just don't cut it anymore. In menswear, patterned ties, jackets and shirts can be seen all at once. Sometimes it works and sometimes it doesn't. In women's wear, we can see a patterned scarf, blouse, and jacket or skirt, and, again, it may work or it may not.

We see the mixture of patterns plenty in hotel rooms or in the pages of *Architectural Digest*; it works and is pleasing to the eye. Guaranteed, whether you notice it or not in these mixtures of patterns, there are some rules being applied. Here are some rules of thumb for you that will be helpful in developing your own signature that is fun and pleasing. When mixing patterns:

1. **Have one dominate pattern and the rest subordinate.** For example, in menswear, your tie needs to be the dominant pattern. If you have a wide striped shirt or chalk-striped suit, you will want to consider a narrow striped tie. If you're wearing a narrow striped shirt, then a wide, regimental striped tie is in order. Just make sure your tie is the dominant pattern.

2. **Have common colors in the patterns.** You can have a patterned blouse, pants and jacket; however, make sure there is a common color throughout. They don't have to match exactly but the color should be present in each pattern.

3. **Have an area in the outfit that is solid to give the eye some rest.** Whether it is the shirt or top or any other component of the outfit, make sure that there is an opportunity for the eye to rest.

Keep Your Wardrobe in Tip Top Shape

As they say with a car, if you don't take care of it, it won't take care of you and get you from Point A to Point B. The same applies to your clothing. If you allow stains to set in and buttons to fall off without replacing them, then you are throwing your money away. The same applies to your shoes. If you allow them to get scuffed and dirty or allow the leather to dry out, how long can you really wear them? Love your clothes and they will serve you well for many years.

The way that clothes are made today, they surely will not last even one season if not cared for. Have you noticed that buttons can come off even after just the first washing? Or perhaps it only takes one washing for that black cotton turtleneck to have a whitish film.

Some things are meant to be dry cleaned and others can be washed at home. Or maybe you don't have time to iron and want that crisp pressed look; taking clothes to the laundry will achieve that. Dry cleaners can be very helpful in keeping your investment; they can sew on buttons and alter clothes if you've lost or gained a few pounds.

Living in a second or third world nation will enlighten you regarding how much you really need to wash or dry clean your clothes. When I was overseas, dryers were not common and my washing machine was hooked up to the kitchen faucet. Given that I lived in a small apartment, when it came time to hanging everything up to dry, my whole apartment was covered. As far as a dry cleaner was concerned, I never found one. So this experience helped me to evaluate the necessity of washing pieces every time I wore them. However, if your clothes have developed an odor, they need to be cleaned. For example, if you're around smokers, your clothes will pick it up a stench. Consider getting a clothing valet to hang your clothes so they can air out over night. If the clothes still have an odor the next day, clean them.

If you're unsure how to clean your clothes, look at the tag it will give the best way to do it. If dry cleaning is recommended, don't do it every time you wear it. Like machine washing, dry cleaning uses chemicals and a rotating cycle that can break down the fabric. Whites become dull, colors lose their vibrant hues, and wools dry out. So get that clothing valet and let the clothes air out, brush them off, and they should be just fine.

Shoes need to be polished periodically and heels and soles need to be redone. Leather uppers sometime tear and need the attention of an expert. For as much as a good pair of shoes cost these days, you'll want to become friends with the cobbler. When we see someone who looks great from head to cuff but has scruffy shoes, it communicates that the individual overlooks the details. For more information regarding care of your clothing investment turn to Chapter 11.

Personal Hygiene Is a Must

This is not just about our hair; it's our teeth and overall cleanliness, too. No matter what work we do, personal hygiene is a must. In America, the norm is to bathe daily, while in other countries that is not the case. However, neither body odor nor bad breath is appealing in any nation! Don't mask body odor with perfumes or colognes; you may just have to bathe more often. If you perspire heavily or live in a humid climate, bathing more than once a day may be the remedy. Consider deodorant with baking soda to absorb underarm stinkiness.

Additionally, cleansing the mouth thoroughly with brushing and flossing will help alleviate food particles from a meal and minimize further problems down the road such as cavities and tooth loss. Brush not only the teeth but also the tongue to remove food and plaque. Consider visiting a dentist regularly to catch problems before they start.

As we age, our mouths get dry – maybe from medication or other reasons. Consider mouth rinses for dry mouth and drinking more water. Consider chewing gum but not in front of customers or clients. As well, our teeth lose their whiteness over years of coffee, cokes and juices, so consider OTC teeth whitening products or having them professionally whitened.

Hair is so much a part of our overall appearance because it communicates our personality, level of personal hygiene, and attention to detail. Make sure to take care of it. Wash it regularly and have it trimmed at least once a month. Short hair needs to be trimmed approximately every three to four weeks and long hair about every six. Seek a style that works with your hair and requires little maintenance throughout the day. Fussing constantly with your hair is counterproductive at work

If you're a man with facial hair, trim it and wash it routinely. Sideburns are fine as long as they are trim and neat. The same goes for a mustache. Be sure to trim it above the upper lip to minimize food particles catching on it – that's not pretty. As a female, facial hair is not something that's desired; hence, consider having laser treatments to eliminate those hairs permanently. Facial hair on women is often a result of a hormonal imbalance that needs medical attention.

Regarding gray hair, both sexes are dyeing it. In fact, coloring products for men are one of the fastest growing sectors in personal care. However, if you're going to color your hair, get some professional advice first regarding a shade that is good for you. When doing it at home, pick a color that is about two shades lighter than your own. Don't try to maintain the same color you had as a young adult; it only ages you. Further, since your hair color is composed of a multitude of shades and highlights seek brands that provide this variation in the formula; this will give a more natural appearance.

Some people have the most gorgeous white hair. Perhaps all they need is a rinse to brighten it. For others, when gray becomes prevalent, the decision to keep it or to color is up to you. Still, if you don't want to color it totally, consider highlights to brighten your natural hair color and thus your complexion. This is an alternative that may work for you.

And if you're losing your hair . . . for men, being bald is quite acceptable. This is your choice; however, if you are losing your hair, don't move the part to the side of your head. That only emphasizes the hair loss. Rather embrace it and have it cut and styled to work with your face shape. For women, hair loss is becoming a major problem. When women enter their 40s, their hair shafts thin and the thick locks we once had can be lost. Sometimes we even experience receding hairlines. When this occurs, seek medical advice or help from your hair dresser. There are options available to help minimize this, such as a different cut, medicine, Rogaine or perhaps a wig.

Conclusion

By understanding the basics to creating a professional appearance you can put your best foot forward in any business culture and excel. These guidelines will shape and guide you in developing your workplace style that communicates your individuality and says that you mean business.

4

The 9 to 5 Dilemma

What will I wear to work? For many, this is a question faced daily. We also think, *While I want to look professional, I also want to be comfortable.* Yes! So given that there are more choices today regarding what we can wear from 9 to 5, let me elaborate on some options that work for Suits Required, Jackets Optional, and Jeans Permitted.

Suits Required

When it comes to wearing suits both men and women are familiar with is formal mode of attire; however, putting this look together is another matter altogether. We've had a lot of education over the years as to what to wear when suits are required, so here are some additional tips to update this look.

For Men: Your work wardrobe will be made up of primarily suits and blazers. Given this understanding, what works and what doesn't is important.

- **If you choose a plaid pattern in a jacket, suit or pant, make sure that the plaids line up the back and side seams as well as the sleeve and shoulders.**
- **When trying on pants, the waist should land right below the navel.** Pants are cut normal or long, so find the best fit for you. If you want them cuffed or plain, that's also up to you.
- **For blazers, you have so many choices; however, you'll want it to cover your derriere.** Consider raw silk, linen blends, in plaids or tweeds with solid colored slacks.

- **For shirts, go for long-sleeved varieties and consider as well pin- or chalk-striped (but avoid plaids).** Make sure that the shirt fabric is of medium weight so it doesn't show everything underneath it. Most times, an undershirt is worn underneath dress shirts for a clean look; make sure the undershirt doesn't show when the collar is open. Consider V-neck styles in T-shirts for a clean look with dress shirts.

- **With dress shirts, there are also a variety of styles to choose from.** If you have an athletic build, go for fitted ones. Regarding the collar, consider the shape of your face and neck. For example, if you have a short wide neck and a full face, consider traditional convertible, tab, or button-down collar styles to balance out the shape. If you have a long neck and an angular face, consider a spread collar.

- **Regarding accessories, you will be tucking your shirt in, and you'll want your belt and shoes to match in color.** Consider brown, cordovan or black. Regarding shoe styles, consider wing-tip, oxford, tie, slip-on and loafer styles with good soles and stable leather uppers. Save the deck shoes for your personal time and, please, no athletic shoes or sandals.

- **Regarding ties, if your work requires a coat AND tie, remember that ties are one of the key accessories for men.** Moreover, the power tie (a red tie) is still in full order, so consider including it as a part of your wardrobe. The width of the tie needs to compliment the width of the lapel.

- **Regarding socks, choose dark colors with subtle patterns and make sure that they stay up on your leg.** A leg exposed when crossed is not pretty.

For Women: Suits and suit separates are going to be the mainstay for your wardrobe. However, today you can kick it up a notch or two. All the restrictions that were apparent in the 70s, 80s and 90s, as well as in the new millennium, have vanished; still, it is continues to be imperative that you look professional. Being sexy and looking it doesn't fly for work. Here are some pointers for **when suits are required**:

- **Consider fabrics and fabric blends that require only easy care and provide comfort, such as wool blended with Lycra** or Spandex, linen polyester blends, Tencel, and cotton/Lycra blends.** Consider woven fabrics over knits for your key pieces; however, double knits that are lined can be very stable and hang well for work. Choose from solids to prints, yet keep the prints subtle.

- **Choose from traditional blazers with a tailor-notched or shawl or mandarin collars when selecting suits and suit separates.** As well consider Chanel style or military styled jackets. Besides blazers and short jackets, consider longer ones that hit below the hip; however, in any choice, seek tailored styles that allow you to switch them out and coordinate with other pieces of your wardrobe.
- **For shirts and blouses, consider tailored shirts or feminine blouses in cotton, silk or polyester blends.** Cowl, jewel, tie or ruffle styles in silk or a fine synthetic soften the face and work with jacket styles; however don't mix totally different styles, like a ruffled shirt with a military styled jacket. Further, make sure that the fabric is not too revealing and there isn't any cleavage showing. Choose from long sleeve, to short sleeve, to sleeveless; however, if wearing sleeveless, wear your jacket at all times. Also, consider sweater sets as an alternative to blouses and jackets.
- **Regarding pants and skirts, consider plain front, or pleated with or without pockets, and those that land at the waist or high hip.** Pants and skirts, with a waist band or not, are suitable. However, if they have a waist band and belt loops, a belt is needed if the shirt or blouse is tucked in. Regarding pant legs, straight or flared is best as opposed to bell-bottom. Fabric choices include tropical weight wools, either in a plain weave or gabardine, that have a great drape. Wear skirts that land at the knee or no more than two to three inches above. Keep longer skirts to about mid-calf.
- **Tailored dresses such as shirt waist styles are an easy option for work in this category.** Consider simple silhouettes with interesting designs, such as princess seams or necklines like a cowl.
- **Regarding accessories consider jewelry in gold, silver and pearls for the most part.** The design is up to you; however, keep it conservative, perhaps a round or angular shape. Small- or

medium- size hoops are fine but they should be in proportion to your size. Have an abundance of scarves to wear at the neck, waist or over the shoulder belted. Accessories are to tie the look together and draw attention to your best asset, your face. Belts are great for long jackets and at the waist for pants or skirts. Also try belting a sheath or two-piece dressing. As well, belt a top and wear it under a jacket. Think about putting a silk kerchief in the breast pocket of your blazer either with the points out or tucked in. Add a broach or pin to the lapel or right above the breast to bring the eye up and to add shine to the face.

- **For shoes, there are lots of options; however, avoid sandals, very high heels and platform styles, and flip-flops.** Consider classic pumps with or without an open toe, loafer or slip-ons, and tailored boots. Seek comfort as well as style with classic designs tailored for your professional image.

Jackets Optional

Some might consider this category "business casual" but really it goes even beyond that. This is an opportunity for men and women to introduce interesting but work-appropriate fabrics, fashion and accessories. Tattoos and body piercings are *not* acceptable and need to be covered. Men and women have lots of options when they don't have to wear a jacket, but one can be added if desired.

For Men: When jackets are optional, it's just as fine wearing a shirt and pants as it is a sport coat and pants. If you need to wear a jacket, you can but it's not mandatory. Here are some ideas and tips to look your best and appropriate at work:

- **Consider twill weave for pants such as Chinos in khaki, navy, olive, black and taupe for starters.** These colors coordinate well with lots of other colors. Choose from cuffed to plain, but realize that when they are cuffed your legs will appear shorter. Choose as well either pleated or plain front pants. Twills come in 100 percent cotton but also there are variety blended with polyester or Lycra for easy care and comfort.
- **As another alternative, consider denim trousers and**

corduroy. Denim trousers are made out of a finer yarn than jeans, and they need to be kept in good condition so they don't look too casual. When they get washed out with holes and fray hems it's time to retire them.

- **Consider as well pants in wool and wool blends in gray, taupe, navy and olive.**
- **Your pants need to land at the waist, and they should be worn with a belt.** Hip huggers are not appropriate.
- **Regarding shirts and tops, consider mock turtlenecks and regular turtleneck styles as alternatives.** Also, consider cardigans, crew and V-neck sweaters worn with or without a jacket. Consider polo tops worn with a blazer or alone paired with twill woven pants such as Chinos. Try also a crew knit top with a blazer or cardigan. Dress shirts, such as button-downs, in solids, stripes or plaids are great choices, preferably in long-sleeves. Consider tartan plaid or vertical stripped shirts worn with either a jacket, a sweater or alone.
- **Avoid fish net, shiny or translucent fabrics for shirts.**
- **Introduce denim shirts that are pressed and clean with tailored lines and wear them either with a sweater, sport coat or blazer.** As well, think about madras plaid shirts worn with trousers.
- **Regarding shoes, consider slip-ons or loafer styles that are tailored but comfortable.** No athletic shoes, sandals or flip-flops, please.
- **Belts need to match the shoe color, and they should be of good leather with a conservative belt buckle.**
- **As well, socks need to match either the color of the pant or the color of the shoe.** Please … no white socks. Choose from a wide variety of subtle patterns that are soft but also wick away moisture.
- **Jewelry should be kept to a minimum.** Regarding earrings, keep them discreet if they are acceptable.

For Women: As we move along the continuum of dressing options for today's office, there are many opportunities to integrate your individual style when jackets are optional. Look to fabrics that are blended with spandex for comfort; however, please avoid 100 percent spandex or your workout outfit. Include single jersey knits that are opaque rather than revealing in tops and skirts. Consider knits in interesting patterns in tops to draw attention to the face in turtleneck, V-, crew -, or boat neck styles. Here are some other suggestions when jackets are optional:

- **Fitted shirts worn with trousers, city shorts or skirts.**
- **Gathered skirts that land at the mid-calf, worn with a blouse and belted.**
- **Introduce cardigans and vests worn with denim shirts.**
- **Layer looks with tank tops and shirt, camisoles and blouses.**
- **Introduce jean jackets worn with trousers, skirts or city shorts.** Include novelty styles as well as those that are more refined with jeweled buttons. Consider ones that are not torn and bleached, and include a variety of colors of these jackets in your wardrobe such as white, black and blue.
- **Include blouses and shirts with a ruffled placket down the front or at the collar worn with a cardigan or blazer.**
- **Wear city shorts that land no more than three inches above the knee with a jean jacket, blazer or cardigan.**
- **Accessorize for impact.** Introduce belts over tunics, scarves in a variety of lengths and sizes. For example, take a long rectangular scarf and wrap it around the neck. It pulls a look together and keeps your neck warm. Or try a large square and wear it over your shoulder, over your blouse and belted.
- **Try some novelty fabrics that are no-iron and extremely comfortable.** An example would be an acetate and spandex blend found in the signature brand of Chico's Travelers. Also incorporate suede and leather in tops and bottoms.
- **Try military styles with epaulets and other details in shirts and jackets.**
- **Introduce feminine and tailored styles together for an appropriate look for work.** Rather than straight pastel jackets and skirts, consider these colors in muted tones such as cadet blue, or wear pastels in small amounts teamed up with a neutral. For example, a muted pink sweater set with gray pants.

- **Try tailored pieces with beading in small amounts, such as a jacket with beading on the shoulders.**
- **Avoid tops with open backs and sheer fabrics.** If you do wear a sheer blouse, put a tank top or camisole underneath. Work is not the place to show what you have.
- **As well, avoid skirts with side slits up the legs.** Rather, consider pencil skirts with a three- to four-inch slit in the back. Consider having your skirts lined so you don't have to wear a slip.
- **Introduce dress silhouettes, such as a shift or sheath, with interesting neck lines such as keyhole or cowl.**
- Shoes should be comfortable, and they can include open-toed pumps, loafers, slip-ons, T-strap and traditional pumps. Stay away from flats, skimmers and the roll-up variety. Also, consider boots to take it up a notch. Avoid athletic shoes and sandals, as well as high platforms and flip flops.

Jeans Permitted

Jeans, which include some of our favorite clothes, are comfortable, and they can work hard. However, when it comes to jeans for the workplace, make sure they are in excellent condition – no holes or tears, frayed hems, acid wash or bleaching. Consider jeans in a dark wash, and when they start looking worn, get another pair for work.

For this category, the emphasis for the workplace is clothing that is clean, conservative and not revealing. Avoid fashion extremes as well. In this category if you want to wear a jacket with your jeans do so. If you don't want to wear jeans you have a multitude of options available and can communicate your individual style succinctly. However, remember that dressing to work is just that, dressing for work and conforming to what is appropriate for your workplace.

For Men:
- **Consider jeans and a denim shirt that is pressed and clean.** However, when it comes to a jean style, avoid hip huggers as well as the low cut variety. Try those that fit at the waist. Choose from a straight, flared or boot cut jean, and avoid skinny or bell bottom varieties.
- **Consider sport shirts and bowling shirts worn out rather**

than tucked in. Usually shirts that are cut straight across are meant to be worn out. There are also styles of shirts that have a minimal tail that allows them to be worn out or tucked in.

- **Consider tailored khakis worn with a Hawaiian shirt or a nice T-shirt without any writing.** Wear the T-shirt tucked in with a belt. Put a denim shirt or cardigan over the T.
- **Regarding accessories, consider fabric belts, such as military style in neutrals such as khaki, navy or olive.** For shoes, consider deck or boat shoes, unless you work on a boat then definitely boat shoes.
- **Consider polo tops tucked into twill fabric pants in neutral colors with a coordinating belt.**
- **Another style of pant to consider is cargo pants.** However, make sure that they are pressed and clean and not the ones that you wear for your personal time. Keep the detailing to a minimum. If shorts are ok try Bermuda styles that land around the knee.
- **Regarding jewelry, keep it to a minimum as well, and wear what is acceptable, such as a wedding band and a watch.** If you want to wear a gold chain, make sure that you wear a single modest short chain around the neck. Avoid heavy gold and silver jewelry – period. If earrings are acceptable, keep them discreet.
- **If you wear a uniform, often they will provide the top and bottom but you'll need to supply the belt.** Make sure that it coordinates with your uniform and is in good condition.
- **You might consider jeans with an oxford, button-down long sleeved shirt in white, blue or a variety of colors.** Make sure that the shirt is tucked in and a belt is worn.
- **Other shoe styles that are good for work include loafers and slip-ons.** Choose styles that are comfort-oriented, yet with stable leather uppers. A tie style with a comfort sole and leather uppers are also appropriate and need to be kept in top shape.
- **Retailers like Target have an employee dress policy that mandates a red top with khaki bottoms but they do not supply them.** Go with a solid polo top with a pair of khaki twills belted and worn with slip-ons. Make sure that you have more than one top and bottom for your work; that way, each day your clothing can be clean and pressed.

- Consider plaid sport shirts worn with v- or crew-neck sweaters and solid colored twill-fabric pants.
- **Introduce suede or synthetic suede, corduroy and other interesting fabrics in tops.** Avoid shiny and translucent fabrics since they are more appropriate for evening. As well, solid colored Ts, in a good weight that doesn't show through, work well. If they start to fad or are wrinkled, wear them during your time but not at work.
- **Consider denim shirts worn with a jacket or vest and solid color twill-fabric pants or jeans.**
- **Tattoos need to be covered, if possible.** Further, any piercings outside of the ears need to be removed for work.

For Women:
- **Jeans need to land at the waist or slightly below. Choose classic styles.** Avoid fashion jeans that can be acid-washed, torn, ripped or have lots of detail. As well, avoid hip huggers or low-cut pants and skirts.
- **Tops can include solid or patterned tunic tops, teamed with a short jacket such as a bomber style that coordinates**.
- **It's important to accessorize your look for the workplace, so consider belts, minimal jewelry and scarves.**
- **If you have piercings in your nose or mouth, take them out.** Keep piercings to one or two pair of earrings per ear.
- **Consider cotton/spandex tops, in a variety of solid colors, layered and worn with crops, trousers, or city shorts that land no more than 3 inches above the knee.** The tops need to be heavy enough so that you can't see through them and have ample ease throughout.
- **Consider a draped cardigan belted with a shirt or blouse, teamed with solid colored pants.**
- **Consider twill-fabric pants or skirts that are classically styled.** In most cases, these will need to be belted if they have belt loops.
- **Introduce layered tops worn with a jean jacket and solid colored bottoms.** For example try layering a couple of T-shirts or tank tops in coordinating colors for a pleasing look.
- **If you work for a company like Target (that calls for an**

employee uniform but does not provide for it), make sure to have several tops classically styled.** These tops can include button down, tailor notched color shirts or crew neck styles, teamed with solid colored skirts or pants. Make sure to have several devoted for the workplace and that they are in great condition.

- **Consider sweaters, either as a pullover or tunic style, worn over a shirt and belted.** Team it up with pants or a pencil skirt or a longer one that lands at mid-calf.
- **Consider tailored cargo pants in neutrals belted or try cropped pants in solids.**
- **Avoid sundresses, see-through tops (unless a camisole or cotton top is worn underneath), tight apparel and exposed midriffs.** No cleavage please.
- **Regarding shoes go for comfort and consider classic styles, such as loafers and slip-ons, tie-ups and boots.** Avoid very high-heels, platforms, flip-flops and sandals. If athletic shoes are OK, consider those with minimal detail.
- **Avoid fashion extremes, fish nets and other designed hosiery, and seek a clean look.**
- **If your employer gives you a uniform, keep it in tip top shape.** Make sure that it fits correctly and keep accessories such as jewelry to a minimum. Avoid wearing rings on every finger.
- **Regarding fabrics, avoid brocades, gauze, sheer and shiny types.** Try suede, corduroy and leather but avoid leather or suede pants. Rather, choose a skirt in these fabrics.
- **Tattoos need to be covered, if possible.**

Conclusion

Today, dressing for work has lots of options, from very formal in a suit to very informal with jeans. Realize that you want to communicate your professionalism and expertise instantly because others will be looking at your appearance as a sign of that. As well, no matter what your occupation and position, your work clothes are not the same as your "play" clothes. Keep them in great shape. I will be covering how to take care of your clothes in Chapter 11. But, for now, look good no matter what the job calls for.

5

If Work Goes Beyond Five O'Clock

Sometimes "work" crosses over into after 5:00 PM with events involving clients, employees or potential customers. So what should you wear when representing your company perhaps doing charity work, as many corporations now do? Anytime that the event involves your company, whether for charity work, a convention or conference, a special event or an employee party, your appearance is just as important. Not only are you driving home the company's image, but yours as well.

Many people feel that the company party or picnic is a time to reveal themselves. *Not quite.* Yes, it's a time to relax and mingle with co-workers. However, it's not a time to get plastered and tell a few things to your boss! So when it comes to dress, this is not an opportunity to wear your own thing. Instead, wear what you wear to work but with some casual aspects if it's a picnic or an office party. So if jeans are appropriate, wear your good jeans and stay away from the designer versions that are holy, torn and/or bleached. For women, no cleavage, spandex tank dresses and thigh-high skirts or slits. For both sexes, avoid wearing all your jewelry (including body piercings) that you normally wear with your friends.

So when it comes to "after five," let's first cover the definition of terms often found in invitations and the attire that they're requesting. Often, under the formal category, there are lots of different levels of formality with different requirements.

Note: If you have to attend lots of black tie affairs, consider investing in a black tux or a dark suit (for men) and either an evening suit or cocktail dress (for women). A great place for cocktail dresses at all price points is www.edressme.com.

Formal Occasions

It's always nice to get invited to a formal affair such as a charity ball or professional gala, but what do you wear? There are plenty of terms used to describe the type of attire desired at a formal function now let's look at those terms for their various interpretations:

- **White Tie:** For men, a white dinner jacket, black pants, shirt and tie or tails. For women, it's a long evening gown in perhaps chiffon, organza or taffeta.
- **Black Tie:** For men, a black tux, shirt and tie, and a cummerbund. For women, long gowns or cocktail dresses.
- **Creative Black Tie:** Perhaps a black tux, black shirt and NO tie (for men). Long or short evening gowns or cocktail dresses (for women).
- **Formal:** Men, it's a tux with no tie. Women, long gown or short cocktail dress.
- **Business Formal:** Black tux, no tie (for men). Tailored dressy evening suits (for women).
- **Daytime Evening Formal:** Usually, this means a dark suit (for men) and a cocktail dress or dark suit or evening separates (for women).
- **Semiformal:** This is usually an event after 6 PM. For men: wear a dark suit or dark blazer. For women: Choose a cocktail dress, or evening separates.

Casual Occasions

If the invitation has the word "casual" in it, here are some of the variations and their interpretations. Bottom line: you will want to make sure that your clothing is clean, pressed, coordinated and accessorized. If jeans are in the picture, go with those that are tailored with a dark wash. Further, when it comes to events that are for your work, sexy attire or fashion extremes are not appropriate.

- **Dressy Casual:** Usually, this means a sport coat and trousers (for men) and tailored separates (for women).
- **Resort Casual:** Includes Hawaiian or leisure shirts worn out and trousers, or a sport coat and trousers (for men), and breezy tops and pants or day dresses (for women).

- **Smart Casual:** Usually, this means a sport coat (for men) and tailored separates (for women).

Putting it Together for any Event

The most important tip to remember regarding any event is to put your best foot forward. This includes putting together a clothing ensemble that is in good condition, coordinated and accessorized for impact. Here are some additional tips for dressing for work when it's after five and beyond:

- **When the event is black tie, men will need to rent a tux or wear a dark (black or navy) suit with a tie.** Some creativity is permitted in the cummerbund and tie, if your corporate culture is less restrictive. However, with the tux, black hosiery and black shoes are a must.
- **For black-tie events, women might look to wearing a short, three-quarter or long dress or gown in silk, chiffon, crepe, taffeta or organza (keep the velvet for the cooler months of October through January).** This is a truly dressed-up event. So look your best and accessorize with appropriate shoes, such as strappy evening sandals in metallic, and ultra sheer hosiery. Include dramatic jewelry and a clutch. Showing up in a lounge suit is not an option. Although tempting, avoid showing off too much cleavage and too much thigh.
- **If attending a professional conference or trade show, the attire you wear for work would be appropriate for this event.** This is where you network and/or meet potential clients or employers. If making a presentation, consider wearing a jacket to distinguish yourself. For men: If the conference is in San Diego, Maui or St. Thomas, Hawaiian shirts are in order for most of the time there; however, bring a blazer and dress shirts for conference banquets. If you're in the advertising industry or similar creative fields, wearing a shirt out with a jacket and good slacks is fine for a banquet. For women: Consider slacks and a fitted shirt or mid-calf skirts and tops. Consider a simple dress with a shawl, or try a matching tunic top and bottom with interesting jewelry for evening banquets.
- **If the conference is overseas, such as in Berlin, Madrid,**

Bucharest or Tokyo, understand that most men and women will be wearing jackets and suits for many events. Even in businesses that are generally more relaxed, such as the tech industry, most industry professionals abroad will lean toward blazers and suits regularly.

- **If the conference runs into the weekend, your appearance is just as important; however, you can dress a bit more relaxed than at work.** Make sure your ensemble is clean and neat and you are coordinated and accessorized.

- **When doing charity for the company**, such as working in a soup kitchen, wear good jeans or other good clothes that will be comfortable while you work. As well, if volunteering with a group like Habitat for Humanity (which builds homes), make sure the clothes you wear will allow you to work, and are clean and neat. Jeans or tops with holes or stains do not communicate a positive image about you or the company that you represent.

- **If you wear a uniform**, you'll often be asked to wear it when working at a remote site for the company. Make sure that it's clean and pressed.

- **How about a charity golf classic?** For men: Consider light trousers or walking shorts in neutrals with polo or golf shirts. Wear appropriate shoes if you're playing, and deck shoes if you're not. For women: Consider walking shorts, polo shirt and flats, with perhaps a sweater depending on the climate.

- **And for an evening function, such as drinks and dinner at TGI Fridays?** Consider nice slacks or your good jeans and a shirt or top. For women consider a skirt, slacks, cropped pants, or good jeans and a conservative top. Make sure to accessorize to complete the outfit.

- **Then there's the more formal dinner or gala.** For men: You would do best with a blazer and slacks or a suit. For women: You might consider a black dress (LBD or the "little black dress") or dressy separates, such as a tunic and pants worn with a great shawl and a dramatic belt.

- **In more traditional fields**, men might consider a dark suit or a blazer and slacks with a dress shirt for the formal dinner. Women will want to introduce bolder jewelry in gold, silver or pearls or an interesting piece that works well with the outfit. It's a great way to get the conversation started.

- **If the invitation says "casual," call the host to find out what that means.** For men: To some, "casual" indicates a sport jacket; for others, it may not. Again, if jeans are permitted, wear your good ones. Consider jeans, a tailored shirt and a jacket. For women: If it's after 6 PM, your outfit might include fabrics such as acetate spandex in a variety of colors in tops and bottoms with an interesting cover. Bottom line: When the invitation says casual, don't equate it with sloppy. In other words, the warm-up suit and athletic shoes won't do.
- **For breakfast and luncheon events during the week, you'll be wearing your clothes for work.**

Going to the Boss's House

- **For men: If invited to the boss's house for dinner, or to watch the Super Bowl, whether you're entertaining clients or not, put your best foot forward.** In businesses where jeans are permitted, consider dark-colored twills like Dockers, that are clean and pressed, topped with a dress shirt tucked in, along with a belt and nice shoes. Even if it's a barbeque, avoid the hoodie, hats, flip-flops, and body piercings, as you would when you go to work. Consider a good pair of jeans and a sport shirt that is pressed.
- **If you're in a business where jackets are optional**, consider dress slacks in a wool or cotton blend with a dress shirt tucked in, a belt and a blazer. Or try a long-sleeve dress shirt with a cardigan or sweater over the shoulders and trousers. If you're invited for the annual Super Bowl party, wear your good jeans and perhaps a turtleneck with or without a blazer.
- **For businesses where suits are required**, a blazer will be in order when clients or potential clients are present at the boss's house. Consider a button-down pinpoint oxford dress shirt with coordinating trousers in gray or taupe. If invited over to watch the Super Bowl or to a barbeque, consider denim trousers and a dress shirt with a V-neck sweater or a polo top and sport coat.
- **For women: If you're invited to the boss's house to entertain clients or prospective clients, or for a barbeque or to watch**

the Super Bowl, consider these options if jeans are permitted at work. When entertaining clients, consider slacks in dark colors with a tunic top belted or a dark skirt with a fitted blouse with a sweater over the shoulder or a nice jean jacket. Consider acetate spandex tops and bottoms with an over-shirt. Make sure to accessorize for impact with earrings and interesting jewelry; however, keep the body piercings at home. For the barbeque or to watch the Super Bowl, consider jeans or a denim skirt with layered tops or a shift. Try a turtleneck with your denim bottoms. Consider boots or sandals but no flip-flops. Try to stay away from strapless sundresses and terry velour fabrics.

- **If in a business where jackets are optional**, consider acetate spandex pants or skirts with interesting tops and jackets for dinner with clients. Consider a dark-colored dress with a shawl around the shoulders. As well, consider a fitted shirt worn out with black pants and a blazer or a mid-calf skirt and an over blouse or tunic belted. For a barbeque or watching the Super Bowl, consider twill pants or skirt with a polo top and a sweater over the shoulders or good jeans with a tunic blouse belted. Consider boots or tie shoes that are in good condition that coordinate. Accessorize with earrings and perhaps a dramatic piece at the neck for impact.

- **If in a business where suits are required**, for dinner at the boss's house with clients, consider a black suit or a black dress. Accessorize with dramatic jewelry and dark sheer hosiery. Choose a simple silhouette with an interesting neck or other detail to speak volumes yet not be busy. Simple elegance is what you're aiming for here. When it comes to the barbeque or watching the Super Bowl, consider trousers or mid-calf skirts, cardigans and turtleneck tops. Or choose an interesting blouse or tailored shirt worn over pants with an interesting belt.

Conclusion

Whatever your business, you can look great for any occasion when it's after five and work-related. These occasions are just as important as during nine to five so give it as much consideration as when you're dressing for work. Look your best, and there will never be the question of whether you're over- or under-dressed for these events.

6

Travel Light and Right

Are you the type of person who brings everything with you when you travel? With airlines charging for bags, you might cut down how much you want to bring on a trip. However, how about when you travel for business? Not only will the time away include business meetings but also evening events in a place where you're not sure how to dress. Perhaps it will be overseas or in another part of the country; how can you pack appropriately in one bag and have everything you need? It's a matter of *planning*.

Rather than stuff your bag with everything you might need, start planning *now* for business travel. It's rather embarrassing when someone is there to pick you up, and you have three bags for a week-long trip. Unless one of those bags is the set-up for the trade booth or merchandise for a trunk show, think ahead and plan accordingly.

When you know you're going to be traveling, look up the *weather forecast* on the Internet. This will help you in deciding what kinds of clothes to bring. Whether traveling overseas or to another state, pack according to the general weather outlook. It won't be right all the time but you'll get a general feeling for the climate. Humid climates, as those commonly found in Florida and Singapore, require some thinking if you perspire easily. If you're traveling to a dry climate, such as in Phoenix or Dubai, the feel of the temperature is very different than a humid one – so think this through. As well, if you'll be working in an air-conditioned setting, such as at a hotel or convention center, and chill easily, that will influence what you pack, too.

Next, figure out your *schedule of obligations,* such as meetings, tours of facilities, sightseeing, dinners, and banquets at these locations.

Consider the level of formality of the corporate culture that you'll be visiting. If it's the company headquarters in New York, you will want to bring either a suit or a blazer. Men consider including a tie or two. Or if you're visiting the company plant in South Carolina (where everyone wears the same uniform from management to the linesperson), then address the informality with a similar ensemble. If traveling overseas to visit with market representatives in London, Paris or Beijing, the business culture is much more formal than in the US so bring a jacket, suit, or suit separates.

Now think about your *luggage*. If you travel frequently, you'll need a good piece of luggage that rolls. If you don't want to check your luggage, it should also be a size appropriate for storage in the overhead compartment of the plane. Consider a 20" Pullman with wheels. Don't expect the luggage you buy to last forever and realize that no matter what it will get beat up, bent and perhaps torn. Luggage can range from a good value to very expensive, depending on what your need is. Consider these tips when making your choice:

- **Purchase luggage with wheels.** Most of us will be handling our own luggage up to the point where we either store it in the overhead compartment or check it in at the airline desk. You have several choices for wheels: *spinners* that rotate 360 degrees, *oversized* that can go over curbs and bumpy roads easily, or the most prevalent, *in-line skate wheels*. Make sure that the wheels are recessed so they don't get torn off.
- **Check out the handles and seek either dual tube or soft handles for comfort, especially if you'll be handling your luggage the most.** Consider luggage with adjustable handles so you can attach a smaller bag easily.
- **Consider fabric when selecting luggage.** Choose a hard-side case if you have valuables to protect or choose from various grades of nylon, such as ballistic nylon, which is extremely strong to your average variety polyester.
- **Make sure the bag has lots of pockets**, on the inside as well as the exterior of the bag, for separating and storing your belongings.
- **If security is an issue where you'll be traveling, have a TSA**

approved lock. Check out their site for more information (www.tsa.gov).

- **Look for luggage that has enclosed spaces to store your liquids.**

Now that we have our luggage, what are some of the things that you'll need to include to make your stay easier for you?

- **If you have a smartphone, does it have GPS?** If not, consider getting one with this feature. It can come in handy. Also, many car rental companies have GPS installed in some cars or allow you to use it for an extra charge. Check with Avis and Hertz.
- **Bring a folded umbrella, just in case.**
- **If traveling overseas, you'll need a voltage converter and an adapter kit of plugs.** If you visit one country extensively, have several of the appropriate plugs so you can charge your phone and/or work on your computer. (Most laptop computers are able to work off of either voltage.)
- **Consider wrinkle release spray.**
- **Have a travel alarm clock or a cell phone that has an alarm setting, if the location does not provide a wake-up call.**
- **Back up your travel documents, including a copy of the itinerary and your passport.**
- **Bring a USB memory stick, otherwise known as a flash drive.** However, may I also suggest having a backup by having the needed files on a cloud website such as www.dropbox.com or others.
- **Copy down any customer-service numbers, such as for the airline or your travel agent.** Also, if your credit card is lost or stolen, you'll need their number to report it.
- **Bring a backup charger, either a plug-in or the battery-operated variety.** Most of us have at least two electronic devices (phone and computer) with us on a regular basis. So be prepared when one of them needs charging particularly if traveling to a country where the electricity is sometimes turned off during the day, a battery-operated charger will be a life-saver; just make sure that it's charged. Always bring extra batteries.
- **If you work out, check out the facilities at your destination**

online to see what's available and pack accordingly. You can't bring all your work-out outfits and shoes, so determine what will work for you for the time away.

Packing Right

When packing, never, never, never stuff your bag!! Your clothes will surely get more wrinkled. To deal with everyday wrinkles in your clothes, you can carry along wrinkle-release spray. Or if you have clothing that is mostly natural fibers, such as wool or cotton, consider hanging them and letting them steam while you're taking a shower. Most hotels will have an iron already in the room or one available through room service; however, if you're not one of those people who will consider steaming or ironing your clothes when they're a bit wrinkled, get the spray. It doesn't matter that you just flew 20 hours to get to your destination; your clothing needs to look clean and pressed.

Here are some more packing tips:

- **Place the things that you'll wear the least at the bottom of the suitcase.**
- **When packing, button your shirts, blouses, cardigans and jackets and fold them at the seams if possible.** For example, when packing jackets in a 20" Pullman, button the jacket, fold the arm sleeves in and then fold the jacket about half and place it in the case width wise. With knits, such as cotton Ts, socks, and pajamas, rolls these and put them where there are gaps to keep your clothes from shifting.
- **When packing toiletries and medication, consider travel sizes that can be purchased at your local grocery or pharmacy.** Repackage and eliminate the extra packaging; however, make sure that you label everything. Have a shave kit or toiletry bag packed at all times so you just need to put it in your bag when you have to leave for a trip.
- **For most jewelry, put what you need in single Ziplock-type bag.** For finer jewelry, get a soft travel case that rolls up. For accessories such as belts, socks, scarves or hosiery, consider putting those in a Ziplock or in a compartment in your bag so everything is together.

- **For pajamas and robes, you know what works for you. However, invest in a travel robe if you're inclined to wear one.** You won't have room for your favorite terry cloth robe.

Travel Basics for Women

When traveling, whatever your occupation or position, bring items that can coordinate with other pieces of your wardrobe. Build your travel wardrobe around neutrals such as black, taupe, camel, navy and go from there. Include lots of accessories, such as scarves, jewelry, belts and hosiery, to change up the look with the same pieces.

Here are some ideas for a great travel wardrobe:

- **If suits are required, bring a suit or suit separates.** Add blouses and shirts for variety and accessorize for impact. Consider a black dress with bold jewelry for evening and stripy sandals. Or consider a dress with a coordinating jacket that works both during business hours and after. Wear the jacket over the dress with some jewelry during the day; take off the jacket and add some bold jewelry and perhaps a shawl for evening. Consider trousers and a coordinating cardigan with a top for weekend events. Choose a couple of pair of shoes, such as pump or ties, that go with your travel wardrobe. Select ones with medium heels.
- **If jackets are optional, consider knits for day and evening wear.** Chico's has their "Travelers" line that was popularized by Michael Phelp's mother during the Beijing Olympics. Made of Lycra spandex and Acetate, they travel well, are easy to care for, and comfortable to wear. Consider pants and skirts and coordinating tops and jackets that can go anywhere as well as day into evening. Good color choices include black, silver, deep navy or dark chocolate. Team up black Traveler's pants with a black turtleneck and jewelry, and perhaps if it's cooler, a tailor mandarin collar jean jacket with jeweled buttons for evening events on the road. For day, try the black pants, belted, with the black denim jacket and a tailored shirt. Everything goes with black.
- **Consider classic suit separates that go from day to evening,**

such a gabardine trousers or skirts and a single blazer in black or navy. Bring an assortment of blouses, shirts and sweaters, such as turtlenecks, that coordinate. Accessorize dramatically for evening events and employ scarves and some jewelry for day.

- **If you have a tendency to get cold in air-conditioned hotels, bring a blazer or good rib-knit or double-knit cardigan.** Pick one that coordinates with the rest of your travel wardrobe.
- **If jeans are permitted, choose ones in a dark wash that are in excellent condition.** Also, pack another pair of pants or a skirt in a neutral, such as khaki or black.
- **Introduce knits, such as sweater sets, cotton V- or round-neck pullovers or turtlenecks, and mock turtle styles.** Look to natural fibers blended with synthetics or 100 percent synthetic fabrics for ease of care.
- **Consider bringing one jacket, perhaps a black blazer or even a cardigan, that coordinates with the rest of your wardrobe.** A blazer or box jacket, if necessary, can take you to evening if jackets are optional and jeans are permitted. Wear it with a silk blouse or jeweled-tone shirt and bold jewelry.
- **Regarding shoes, don't buy any to wear brand new on your trip, or your feet will hate you.** Buy the shoes about a week or two in advance and break them in at home, then they'll be ready for your trip. Consider bringing a pair of shoes, perhaps slip-ons, loafer or tie styles, in a medium to low heel such as an inch and a half.
- **When it comes to cosmetics, have them in a makeup bag.** You may like to use lots of makeup but you can only take what you'll really need. Pick the colors you wear most often. All of my makeup is in such a bag, and this makes it really easy to travel anywhere. It also cuts down on decision-making each morning.

Travel Basics for Men

- **For men, where suits are required, consider bringing a gray suit and a navy blazer with coordinating slacks and shirts.** Double up on your ties and shirts so you have variety each day. Make sure to include coordinating belts and shoes as well as other accessories. For the weekend, consider button-down pin point oxford dress shirts with trousers and a cardigan or pullover with your blazer. Limit shoes to two pairs, such as wing tips, ties or slip-ons.

- **If jackets are optional, you'll want to include a pair of trousers in a neutral, such as gray, khaki or olive.** Wear the trousers with button-down oxford shirts, polo shirts, or long-sleeve plaid shirts, pullover sweaters, v-necks, or turtleneck sweaters that coordinate with a blazer. Bring a sport coat or blazer just in case and confine shoes to loafers and perhaps deck shoes.
- **If jeans are permitted, bring your best pair in a dark wash.** Consider a black or navy blazer for dressier occasions in the evenings. For these, you can wear a white dress shirt, jeans and your blazer. Introduce pullovers, cardigans and short sleeve pullovers tops that coordinate with your jeans.

Some Pointers on Going through Security

- Wear slip-on shoes.
- Wear your blazer (it will give you tons of room in your suitcase).
- If bringing a carry-on bag, the TSA provides tips for packing this so the security agent can see everything quickly if they need to open it. Go to www.tsa.gov.
- **Know the TSA regulations for liquids and have them available.** Basically its 3-1-1 … liquids in containers no larger than 3.4 ounces, one clear quart-size Ziplock bag to put them in, and everything one suitcase. Have the Ziplock bag in the outer compartment of your luggage so you can get it out quickly as you approach security.
- **Make sure all your electronics are out, your pockets are empty, and your jewelry and belts are off.** You'll also have to take off any jackets and scarves.
- **Have your laptop in a TSA-approved carrier, opened and ready to go through the screener.** Go to www.tsa.gov for specifics; however, the carrier should have a laptop only section

that opens and lies flat without inside or outside pockets and no zippers or buckles inside or underneath this side. Moreover, only keep the laptop in this section.

- **Have your boarding pass and ID in your hand.**

Conclusion

In many occupations travel is part of the job description. Even with the internet and face time calling, nothing quite closes a deal than a face-to-face meeting. In this day and age where traveling to another country is commonplace you will now be prepared to go anywhere and be the consummate professional that you are. Happy travels!

7

The Foundation of Style

Being able to dress with style doesn't require hiring a stylist or fashion consultant. Instead, it's about having an understanding of why and how pieces go together. As a fashion design major in college, I had to take a lot of courses in not only pattern-making, design and tailoring, but also in art. There's a lot more involved than simply coordinating an outfit. In addition, fashion requires an understanding of the elements and principles of design so you can be effective in developing a look that's coordinated, aesthetically pleasing, and communicates who you are. If you have an art background, perhaps you took such classes. These elements and principles provide the foundation for successfully designed clothing and being coordinated and stylish. Plus, knowing the tools of the trade will ensure your success in whatever you wear, whether it's Suits Required, Jackets Optional or Jeans Permitted.

The elements of design provide a foundation for developing a style, and they include color, texture, shape or form, line and space. Meanwhile, the principles provide the method for putting the elements together in a pleasing manner. The principles include rhythm, proportion, balance, emphasis, unity and harmony.

The Elements

The elements of design are like the wood boards and nails when building a house. They are the tools, that when used in a pleasing manner creates a beautiful home. Let's discuss each one.

Line

This is one of the simplest and strongest elements of design. Often we don't pay attention to lines but they communicate a lot of meaning. For example, horizontal lines communicate tranquility while vertical ones say tradition. Straight lines communicate rigidity and precision while curved lines suggest gracefulness and femininity. Zigzag lines can be nerve-racking because they force the eye to shift often and abruptly while diagonal lines imply action. Lines can be thin or thick and this can add emphasis to the meaning the lines take.

In clothing, there are two types of lines – *structural* and *decorative.* Structural lines are in the structure of the garment, such as the vertical lines in a pleated skirt or shirt. Or this could be the topstitched line in a dress or the curve line created with a raglan sleeve. Decorative lines are those found commonly in the fabric pattern and other decorative features of the garment, such as buttons and epaulets. Or how about the lines created in a rib knit sweater or the lines present in a chalk-striped jacket? These are structural and decorative lines that communicate meaning, and they are present in garments we wear.

However, what is the look *on you* of the structural horizontal lines created in the neckline with a turtleneck sweater or from the hem of a skirt or jacket? Many times, we're not aware of the many lines that make up an outfit, but take a moment to look at the lines in some of yours. What are the dominant lines present? Items that have straight lines, such as A-line skirts and tailor-notched collar blouses, go together because of the similarity in the straight vertical lines.

Further, you can use line to create an optical illusion. For example, if your body type is very angular, you might want to incorporate curved lines, such as ruffles or floral patterns, to balance your shape. If you're petite, incorporate vertical lines to create an illusion of height, as in high-heel shoes, pin stripes and other structural and decorative lines. If you happen to have a round shape, incorporate straight lines to balance it.

Form

Form is the 3-D version of shape. For example, form takes into account height, width and depth, and it is created when two or more shapes are combined. A shape is what stands out from space; for example, it might be a patched pocket on a jacket or a collar on a shirt. Form can also define a shape or silhouette, such as bell shaped, full or body-conscious, and tubular. Form describes the garment shape and shapes within the garment, and it can express feelings and emotions.

Form can also create illusions. If you're slim and angular, consider incorporating round shapes to balance it. As well, if you're on the heavy side, consider long rectangular shapes and forms to create a slimmer appearance.

Space

Space is the background of the design, and it includes both positive and negative space. To understand this concept, think of a picture of a house amid a beautiful landscaped field. The field is the background or negative space while the house is in the foreground and occupies positive space. In patterned fabrics, for example, the pattern is the positive space while the background color is the negative space. Space is also in the structure of a garment, such as patch or welt pockets, zippers and buttons, and it can enhance the overall form.

Take, for example, a sheath dress; the shape is straight, sometimes tubular. If the fabric is gathered across, what shapes are produced in the folds of the fabric? The folds create the positive space with the background acting as negative space. How about a shift dress silhouette? We can divide the space with a seam down the middle and have one side be one color and the other side another color. We can also add a row of buttons down the front to add dimension as well as creating positive and negative space.

Texture

This element of design enhances our sense of touch and perception. There are cool and warm textures; for example, wool flannel is a warm texture while satin is a cool one. To elaborate, *warm textures* are warm to the touch because light is absorbed by the fabric. They include cotton, raw silk, lamb's wool, flannel nightgowns and corduroy. *Cool textures* are cool to the touch and they reflect light. Examples of cool textures include acetate, polished cotton, satin, lame and taffeta. In coordinating outfits, consider putting together textures that are similar in temperature – as in a sweater set with flannel pants.

However, mixing texture temperatures can create an optical illusion that can balance your body type. For example, if you're larger in the hips than in the top, consider wearing a cool texture on top, such as a polished cotton jacket, with a warm texture bottom. Moreover, a heavy or bulky texture on top with a smooth texture fabric on the bottom will also balance your proportions. As well, if you're very thin, you can create the illusion that you are larger with bulky, warm textures and shiny cool ones. If you're large, concentrate on warm, smooth fabrics, such as woven polyester, worsted wool, and cotton.

Color

Outside of line, color is one of the most important elements of design. It's probably the first thing we think of when coordinating an outfit. As fun as color is, there's a lot worth knowing about this element of light. Yes, color is produced by light. If you remember your science class, you probably worked with a prism and the rainbow produced when light showed through it.

Color is light. Let me explain. When we see a color, what we are seeing is the reflection of the color that is NOT absorbed. So all the colors are absorbed by light, and the color we see is what is reflected. Since color is light, it affects our eyes. Different colors have different wavelengths so when we see different colors, our eyes have to stop and adjust to the difference in wavelength. That is why it's recommended that individuals that are petite wear clothing from the same color family so the eyes do not have to stop and adjust to the different color wavelengths thereby giving a long view of an individual rather than cutting them in half – so to speak.

Let's first focus on the dynamics of color and the associated terminology:

- **Hue** is another name for color.
- **Tint** is a color with white added to it, such as light blue.
- **Shade** is a color with black added to it, such as forest green.
- **Value** is the lightness or darkness of a color; light blue has a higher value than dark blue.
- **Tone** is a color with gray added to it, such a cadet blue or mauve.
- **Intensity** is the purity of a color. When a color is intense or bright, the hue is in its purest form. To dull or lower the

intensity of a hue, add its complement (see "complementary colors" below). For example, the color red alone is in its purest form and therefore intense. When you add its complement, green, it dulls the color and red loses its intensity.

- **Monochromatic colors** are colors from the same color family, like light blue, cadet blue and periwinkle blue.
- **Complementary colors** are opposite one another on the color wheel. The complement of red is green, for yellow it's purple, and for orange it is blue.
- **Analogous colors** are those that are next to one another on the color wheel. For example, orange is analogous to red, blue to green, yellow to orange, and purple to blue. Analogous colors coordinate well together, as do those with contrasting values.
- **Warm colors** make areas advance or appear larger, and they include yellow, orange and red.
- **Cool colors** make areas recede or appear smaller, and they include blue, green and purple.

The Principles of Design

As mentioned before, the principles are the how-to of putting the elements together, and they include balance, proportion, emphasis, rhythm, unity and harmony. Essentially, the principles guide you in putting your outfits together in a pleasing manner that is stylish and coordinated. Let's get started!

Balance

Just like a seesaw, you want to strive for balance in your outfits. The principle of balance suggests that if an imaginary line were drawn down the middle of your outfit, each side would have equal weight. At least that's what you want to strive for. There are two forms of balance, *formal* and *informal*. In formal or symmetrical balance, each side of the imaginary line is the same. For example, when wearing a suit, or a blazer and trousers, each side is the same – with pockets on each side and each trouser leg being the same. Formal balance communicates a feeling of tradition, stability and confidence.

In informal or asymmetrical balance, each side is different but the feeling of the same weight is achieved. This type of balance is considered more interesting and dramatic to the eye than formal balance. Consider a shift dress with a big blue pocket on one side and a small yellow one on the other. A color like yellow is a strong advancing color while blue is receding. Although the two sides are different, the weight is the same. Perhaps you might have on a chain belt with the end hanging to one side, and wearing a scarf, jewelry or a short jacket could achieve informal balance.

Proportion

If you've ever built model airplanes or ships, or perhaps you're an architect now who builds models of buildings, you know that everything has to be to scale. One of the great wonders in the world is the Vatican cathedral in Rome, where everything inside is in proportion to each other – it is magnificent! This same principle applies to apparel. Each part of your clothing ensemble should be in proportion to each other and ultimately to you. For example, a big collar shirt with big buttons with a tiny belt is not in proportion to one another, nor is a big shirt with a scarf that has a tiny pattern. Furthermore, as I said, the components of the garments you're wearing should be in proportion to the wearer. For example, if a larger person wears a tiny belt or a tiny stripe print, these will be out of proportion to their size.

With proportion, we also have to talk about *ratios*. In breaking down the top and bottom of an outfit, you'll want to strive for a *2:3 ratio*. Imagine dividing up your outfit into three equal parts, you would want to have either 2 parts in the jacket and one part in the bottom or one in the jacket and two in the bottom. A 2:3 ratio might be a long jacket with a short skirt or a blazer and trousers. Another example might be a blazer and city shorts or a short jacket and trousers. In a *1:2 ratio*, the top and bottom are equal, as with a long jacket and an equally long skirt. This ratio is not as interesting or appealing to the eye as a 2:3 ratio.

Emphasis

Emphasis is a point of dominance. When putting together an outfit, what is the dominant point of interest? If you have too many points of interest, your outfit will be confusing the eye. Most times, you'll want to draw attention to your best asset – your face – so incorporate accessories to lead the eye up. However, when putting an outfit together well, a woman might choose an interesting necklace or belt but not both. If it's the belt, then she could put a subtle piece around the neck. For men, creating this point of emphasis might include the belt, a kerchief in the breast pocket or a tie to draw the eye up to the face.

Emphasis can be achieved through contrast in size, color, texture, line or shape of an apparel item or accessory. To find out what the point of emphasis is, take a quick look in the mirror – what catches your eye first is the point of emphasis. Work on having a single point of emphasis and have the rest of the outfit and accessories support this point but not fight for first place.

Rhythm

Rhythm in style/fashion is like rhythm in music, it's that constant, repetitive beat that keeps the music going at the same tempo. In dress, rhythm ties the outfit together, and it includes repetition in color, texture, shape, form or line that creates a unified feeling. It can be the progression or gradual increase or decrease of similar colors, shapes, lines or textures in an outfit.

When coordinating outfits, repeating the color, line, texture or shape pulls it together. For example, a woman could try combining a tailored skirt that has a lot of straight lines with a blouse that also has a lot of straight lines – like a pleated front style. In menswear, repeating a pattern or color in the shirt or tie pulls the look together. Adding a pocket square that repeats the color is another way.

As mentioned, progression is another way to achieve rhythm in an outfit that is coordinated. An example of progression would be wearing a light blue shirt and darker blue pants. This is also called a monochromatic color scheme where variations of a single color family are worn.

Unity

As it sounds, when you're putting an outfit together, you want it to look unified. Are all the pieces there? When you look in the mirror, is there something missing – like a belt or jacket? It's when you feel that something's missing, that the outfit is not unified. For example, if you wear a shirt and slacks alone, the outfit is not unified. Pull it together with accessories, such as jewelry, a belt, a scarf or hosiery for women.

This principle is just as important for men as it is for women, with key pieces needed to pull the look together such as a belt or pocket square.

Harmony

As important as unity is, so is harmony. Like harmony in music, harmony in apparel suggests commonality in color, line, shape and form, and texture. However, too much harmony creates monotony. For example, if you wear a tailored jacket, shirt and pants in variations of blue, you need to add something different to create interest. A man might try a pocket square with a curved pattern to add interest, and a woman, a scarf with a floral pattern. Another example for a woman might be a tailored skirt and blazer, and wearing a ruffled blouse for interest.

Conclusion

Understanding why and how clothing goes together will helpful to you. You'll be able to create new and appealing outfits that are appropriate for work and reflect who you are. Now you don't need a stylist. With this information, you are the stylist for your great look!

8

Make Color Work for You

Color is a very important aspect of our lives. When we go shopping, what attracts us first to a sweater or jacket? Might it be the color? Color influences our emotions. For example, red ... especially in a red fire truck, our blood pressure goes up when we see it and we get excited. In fact, red influences us physically more than any other color. Here's another example of color's influence on our emotions; when we are sad, sometimes we wear bright colors to make ourselves feel better.

Color marks events throughout the world and it communicates many messages. In China, for example, red is considered a very lucky color. During Lent before Easter, many churches drape alters in purple fabrics and wear the same color garments. Brides usually wear white at their wedding and many people were black or dark colors at a funeral. Color is also used to identify groups of people, such as those hues worn by the teams at a soccer match. And students attending a specific school could identify themselves by wearing their institution's colors.

As we learned in the previous chapter, color is one of the most important elements of design, and it is a product of light absorption and reflection. As well, color has many facets, such as tints, shades, pure hues, complementary and analogous colors as well as monochromatic color schemes. Since color plays such a major role in our daily lives, it is important to learn how to benefit by it. Color can compliment your skin color or work against it. It can also help to create an optical illusion when used in apparel to balance your body to make it appear in proportion. Color can also be used to compliment your personality and help you to project the professional image you want.

Colors and Their Meanings

Let's look at the meaning of various colors. These meanings are not universal. Colors may mean something totally different in another country, so please be mindful of this variation if you travel for business outside of the United States.

The meaning of color:

- **Red:** Hot, dangerous, angry, passionate, sentimental, exciting, vibrant and aggressive.
- **Orange:** Lively, cheerful, joyous, warm, energetic, hopeful and hospitable.
- **Yellow:** Bright, sunny, cheerful, warm, prosperous, cowardly and deceitful.
- **Green:** Calm, cool, fresh, friendly, pleasant, balanced, restful, lucky, envious and immature.
- **Blue:** Peaceful, calm, restful, highly esteemed, serene, tranquil, truthful, cool, formal, spacious, sad and depressed.
- **Purple:** Royal, dignified, powerful, rich, dominating, dramatic, mysterious, wise and passionate.
- **White:** Innocent, youthful, faithful, pure and peaceful.
- **Black:** Mysterious, tragic, serious, sad, dignified, silent, old, sophisticated, strong, wise, evil and gloomy.
- **Gray:** Modest, sad and old.

Tips for Using Color

When dressing for work or anything else, color becomes a significant factor in your choice. If you wear too many colors in an outfit, the ensemble appears gaudy. However, use too little and your clothes seem drab. Seek a good balance, perhaps a maximum of three different colors. This is a good number whether putting together your outfit for work or anything else.

Here are some additional tips when dressing for work and other occasions.

- **When it comes to formal events, *black* is the best color for your attire.** It's sophisticated and slimming. Consider a tuxedo in black or a black cocktail dress.

- *Brown* **and its variations are popular in the mid- and southwest because they mimic the colors found in the landscape.** Think about using variations of brown, such as dark chocolate, cinnamon, gray brown, or wheat, in your work wardrobe.
- *Navy* **is a great color for every complexion.** And as you age, it becomes a more suitable color than black; it's not as severe against your skin color. Navy is commonly seen in resort wear, and in nautical apparel, because of its associations with water and the coast.
- *Beige* **and** *gray* **communicate professionalism and elicit a feeling of group authority and acceptance.** In contrast, navy communicates the feeling of individual authority.
- *White* **is best accessorized with other colors.** It is usually not worn for work, except as shirts and blouses. Rather than white such as a doctor's coat, consider winter white, a creamy white, for suit separates at work.
- *Red, green* **and** *blue* **in assorted tints and shades are suitable for all occasions, especially work.** Consider such variations as burgundy, forest green, or cadet blue in your wardrobe. Pastel versions of these hues are also found in the workplace, primarily in shirts, blouses and sweaters.
- *Yellow* **is great for casual apparel; however, don't forget variations of this hue for the workplace.** Colors such as golden or mustard work well for ties, shirts, jackets and tops.
- **Bright colors, such as** *fuchsia* **and** *turquoise,* **are often seen in coastal cities like Miami.** They also provide a great accent to your work apparel. Team them up with neutrals for balance and excitement.
- **Dark, cool and dull colors make forms appear smaller.** If you want to look 10 pounds/kilos smaller, wear these colors. Consider black, charcoal gray, dark chocolate, burgundy, purple and olive to make large areas appear smaller.
- **Light, warm and bright colors make objects appear larger.** Consider incorporating yellow, white, orange, red and bright colors in parts to balance small areas of the body.

- **If you are shy, try wearing red to be perceived as more assertive.**
- **If you're perceived as strong and aggressive, wear cooler tones such as navy and gray as well as beige to be perceived more approachable.** As well, if you're tall and big-framed, consider these colors to come across more personable rather than intimidating to others.

Color has such an impact on our lives regarding our emotions and how others see us. Incorporate color in your wardrobe and let it work for you.

Color & Skin Tone

Another aspect of color is wearing those that enhance or compliment your skin tone. Wearing the right colors does make a huge difference in how the color of your skin, eyes and hair come across. As we age, we lose color in our face, hair, eyes and lips. The colors that we wear need to also change to reflect this evolution. At a later stage, tints and shades, rather than pure hues, might be considered in clothing choices.

As well, when we decide to change our hair color, this will influence the color of our skin and the best colors to wear. Do get the advice of a professional when you decide to change your hair color. If you are graying and you want to color your hair, consider choosing a shade that is at least two shades lighter than your natural color. Also, seek one that is either cool or warm to match your skin tone. For example, if you have an olive complexion, your skin tone is cool; your choice for hair color should also be cool, such as burgundy, ash blonde, or ash brown.

Skin colors vary from one individual to the next; however, most can be categorized into either *cool* or *warm*. Cool skin tones, such as olive, have blue undertones. This is evaluated by considering the closeness of the blood vessels to the surface of the skin. With cool skin tones, the blood vessels are close to the skin's surface. In contrast, with warm skin tones, the vessels are deeper into the skin and not as obvious.

Because of this factor, some colors look better on cool skin tones than warm. However, with all the colors, there are warm and cool versions. For example, with the color blue, you might find a blue with yellow added, such as turquoise or teal, that is great for warm skin tones.

Meanwhile, blue with purple added is wonderful for cool skin tones. As well, with the color red, red with more blue added is better for cool skin tones while red with yellow added is better for warm. Nonetheless, if a certain color makes you feel good or you get many compliments when having it on, WEAR it.

The next sections will provide guidelines to aid you in picking colors that work well with your skin.

Winter

If you're part of the winter family, you have cool undertones in your skin, and you're part of a very, very large family. The majority of people fit into this category, which includes most Asians, Latinos and Blacks. I'll break it down by skin, hair and eye color and also provide the colors that work best for you.

Skin: Blue or blue-pink undertones, very white, beige, brown, rosy beige, olive, black with blue undertones, or charcoal brown freckles

Hair: Blue-black, medium brown, dark brown, salt and pepper, silver gray, white blond and white.

Eyes: Dark red-brown, black-brown, hazel, gray blue, blue with white flecks in the iris, dark blue, gray-green and green with white flecks in the iris.

Colors that work best: Navy, black, shocking pink, purple, taupe, burgundy, chartreuse, red, white, gray, chocolate brown, blue, forest green and blueberry.

Summer

Summer skin tones also have cool undertones. Look for colors that are blended with cooler colors, such as green, blue and purple.

Skin: Blue undertones, pale beige with pink cheeks, pale beige, very pink, rosy or charcoal brown freckles, gray-brown.

Hair: Platinum blonde, ash blonde (grayish cast), dark brown (taupe tone), brown with an auburn cast, blue-gray and pearl white.

Eyes: Blue with brown around the pupil, gray-blue, gray-green, pale gray, blue with white flecks, green with white flecks, hazel, bright clear blue, pale clear aqua and soft brown.

Colors that work best: Soft blues, navy, plum, lavender, ice beige, slate gray, taupe, dusty coral, rose pink, mauve, rose-brown, blue-gray, sea blue, raspberry, pale green and sea foam.

Spring

Springs have warm undertones, with some having more yellow or peach in their skin tone. The blood vessels are not as close to the surface, as with cool undertones.

Skin: Golden undertones, ivory, ivory with pale golden freckles, peach, golden beige and rosy cheeks.

Hair: Flaxen blonde, golden blonde, strawberry blonde, auburn, golden brown, red-black, and golden gray.

Eyes: Blue with white rays, clear blue with brown flecks, aqua, bright blue (turquoise), light golden brown, clear green and teal.

Colors that work best: Golden brown, camel, peachy pink, ivory, marine blue, bright green, aqua, tangerine, cream, peach, soft blues, golden yellow, periwinkle, coral, turquoise, soft yellow and jade.

Autumn

Autumn skin tones also have the warm undertones that come with the blood vessels being deeper into the skin.

Skin: Golden undertones, ivory, ivory with freckles, peach sometimes with freckles, golden beige, dark beige (copper colored), and golden brown.

Hair: Red, coppery red-brown, chestnut brown, golden brown, charcoal black, golden gray and auburn.

Eyes: Dark brown, golden brown, amber, hazel (golden brown), green (brown or gold flecks), pale clear green, or blue with aqua tones.

Colors that work best: Turquoise, orange, gold, emerald, mustard, dark brown, sea blue, clay, banana, royal blue, cream, teal, brick red, moss green, camel, gold, warm beige, olive, celadon, butterscotch, ivory and salmon.

If you like a color, but it's not recommended for you, wear it as a jacket or pants but avoid it next to your neck and face. For example, I'm a winter and should not wear salmon. However, I love the salmon color. So when I wear my salmon pullover, I wear a white polo shirt underneath it so the white rests next to my neck and face. Or women could wear the color as a top, and pull the look together with a scarf that has the colors good for their skin tone. They would drape the scarf next to their skin. For men, consider as well wearing a favorite color as a pocket square, tie, or another type of accessory, such as cardigan or vest.

Conclusion

Color is light and affects our moods. When we wear colors we like we feel good which ultimately affects our interactions with others. By using the guidelines presented in this chapter you can wear colors in confidence knowing that you will look great at the office or wherever the day may take you.

9

Maximize Your Assets, Minimize Your Liabilities

If everyone was a "10," we wouldn't need Photoshop! Even models and celebrities have their figure flaws; however, they camouflage them well with the clothes they wear. There was recently a commercial for Dove where they showed a woman from the very beginning to the final processed photo; the change was so dramatic that I wondered if the model even recognized herself!

No one has the perfect measurements or is proportioned according to some standards. Why should we even follow someone else's standards! However, if you don't like something about yourself, understand that the way that you wear your clothing can help to minimize those liabilities and maximize your assets. A lot of it has to do with what we talked about earlier with the elements of design. By understanding how the elements work, you can achieve the desired look – either through line, form, color, texture and space. For example, if you're thin and angular, wear curved lines and shapes as well as warm colors and heavier textures. As well, if you have a long neck, wear shirts with collars and light-colored turtleneck tops that help put the neck in proportion to the rest of your body. How about if you're bowlegged? Consider longer, fuller skirts if you're a woman and full-cut slacks if you're a man. Although skinny jeans may be all the rage, wearing those will only point out a bowed shape.

I have measured myself but to be honest I haven't done so lately. But one thing is for sure, I do know that I am like so many women in the world; I am larger on the bottom than I am on top. Guaranteed, this is common among men as well because gravity works its wonders over the years. Unless you exercise vigorously, have plastic surgery, or just have been graced with a top that is larger than the bottom, most of us will have to deal with our lower half being larger than our upper half. In this chapter, I will share with you some insights for both men and women on how to minimize your liabilities and maximize your assets. Since men and women are different; I will present each separately.

For Women

Wearing a body stocking or bra and panties, measure across the bust, waist and the fullest part of the hips. Next, measure from the top of the head to the bust, from the bust to the fullest part of the hip, from the hip to the middle of the kneecap, and from the kneecap to the floor. Also, measure your neck length and the diameter of your wrist and ankle. Note your height and weight and observe the shape of your shoulders. Are they broad and straight with little slope or tapered and/or very sloped.

To determine whether you are short- or long-waisted , use the measurement from your bust to your hip and your hip to your knee. Ideally these two measurements should be the same. However, if your bust-to-hip measurement is longer than your hip-to-knee measurement, you are long-waisted. If it is shorter, then you are short-waisted, yet probably have long legs. To further determine leg length, the measurement from head to your bust and from your knee to the sides of your feet should be about the same. If the head-to-bust measurement is shorter than the knee-to-feet measurement, you probably have long legs. However, if the head-to-bust measurement is longer than the knee-to-feet measurement but your hip-to-knee measurement is shorter than your bust-to-hip, you probably have high hips, short thighs, and long calves.

Some rules of thumb to go by are that you want your bust and hip measurement to be about the same while the waist is about eight inches smaller. The circumference of the upper thighs should be about the same size as the waist.

So what did you find out? Besides just succumbing to the tape measure results, take a look in the mirror. What do you see? What do you feel is not ideal TO YOU? Don't think about what you see in the magazines; they have been airbrushed and modified. Now let's look at how you can use clothing to play up what you like and play down what you don't.

- **If an ample derriere is your figure flaw, make sure pants fit properly.** Pants should fit smoothly and loose enough over the thighs that the fabric flows from the fanny to leg without pulling. Also, avoid tight fitting, box-style jackets since they only accentuate this liability; rather, choose a longer styled jacket such as a blazer, but not oversized that might shorten your leggy image.
- **However, if you lack a shapely derriere, choose styles with fullness in the back, such as gathered skirts.** Consider layers of fabric in the back, as in jackets with gathered backs or pleated backs that add fullness to this area. Or try two-piece outfits with overlapping tops and avoid drop-waist styled fashions altogether.
- **Does your stomach stick out?** To minimize this, make sure that skirts and pants fit properly. Avoid hip hugger pants but perhaps consider pants that land about one inch below the waist. Consider plain front as opposed to pleated pants and skirts since they only add extra fabric to that area of the body. Also consider empire waist dresses and tops as well as pants and skirts with side-slash pockets. Don't cinch your waist in with belts, rather consider chain belts worn loosely below the waist with the closure toward the side.
- **If you have wide hips, make sure that pants and skirts fit properly.** Consider drawing attention to the center and to your face with a front placket with buttons or similar design down the front. Avoid back pockets in pants and jeans, straight skirts, and jackets and tops that end at the widest point of your hip. Avoid borders and any horizontal stripes around the hip region and try boot-cut or flared pants to balance your body. Consider jackets that land at the waist or shorter to build up the upper body so you look proportioned.
- **If your thighs are heavy, consider A-line skirts or dresses.** Make sure that pants and skirts fit properly and smoothly over the thighs. Consider boot-cut or flared bottom pants to balance

out the thighs. If you like shorts, wear city, walking or Bermuda length styles. Wearing short shorts puts the horizontal line of the hem of the shorts at your thighs and makes them appear larger. In pants, avoid any detail at the thigh, such as patch pockets, rather consider styles that have more detail below this area.

- **If your legs are short, avoid cuffed pants and consider pants with vertical stripes.** Wear high-heeled shoes and high-waisted styles to give a leggier image. Avoid long skirts since they will only accentuate short legs. Consider skirts that fall no less than 3 inches above or at the knee to make your legs appear long.

- **If your legs are long, avoid high-waisted styled skirts and pants and wear cuffed trousers.** Consider tunics and drop-waisted fashions to put those legs in proportion with the rest of your body. Try contrasting colored tops and bottoms and jackets that are slightly longer with one or two button closings. Avoid vertical stripes in pants and skirts.

- **If your waist is wide, consider wearing dark colored belts that draw the waist in.** Or perhaps consider dresses with princess seams that also give you a waist. You might consider wearing layers to hide your waist altogether as in shirts worn out with vests or blouses worn out with a cardigan.

- **If you're large busted, avoid short sleeves, high-waisted styles, low yolks and the use of horizontal lines at the bust.** As well, avoid cinching in your waist with a belt; rather choose V-neck, with or without lapels, and vertical lines in the fabric design or structure of the garment. Try three-quarter or long sleeve tops with any detail away from the bust area. Wear pants with flare legs to help balance the top.

- **However, if you're small busted, avoid blouse designs and necklines that expose the cleavage or cling to the skin.** As well, look for jackets and shirts that have patch pockets or other detail at the breast area and give it extra weight. Consider bras that are padded and enhance what you have, such as the Wonderbra by Victoria's Secret.

- **If your shoulders are wide avoid boat neck style tops and**

epaulets. Sloping or narrow shoulders benefit by padding in the shoulders as well as V-neck style tops and jackets.

- **If you're petite or average and want to appear taller or longer, emphasize vertical lines in your wardrobe selections.** Vertical lines can be found in the fabric pattern or in the structure of the garment, such as pleats, vertical darts and princess seams. Choose high-waisted skirts and trousers and short, waist-length jackets such as Chanel or bomber styles. Consider hemlines that fall at the knee or no more than 3 inches above it. Wear heels and consider V-neck styles in blouses and tops. As well, consider wearing a single color or a monochromatic color scheme in the top and bottom; that way, the eyes will flow from top down without stopping.

For Men

Dressed in your underwear, measure yourself at the chest, the fullest part of the hip, and the waist. Also measure across the back at the shoulders, and measure your neck length and diameter, as well as the diameter of your wrist and ankle. Take the length from the top of your head to the middle of the chest, from the chest to the fullest part of the hip, from the hip to the middle of the knee, and from the middle of the knee to the floor. Note your height and weight as well as the shape and width of your shoulders. Are they broad and square, broad and tapered, or medium and sloped?

The distance from the top of your head to your chest should ideally equal the distance from the middle of the kneecap to the soles of the feet. The length from the middle of chest to the fullest part of the hip and from the fullest part of the hip to the middle of the kneecap should also be equal. Variations of these lengths will determine whether you are short- or long-waisted and if you have short or long legs. For an athletic-build body, the average drop in inches from the chest to the waist is seven inches or more.

Now what did you find out? Whatever it is, now you know and can dress and shop for yourself much more efficiently and effectively. We all have figure flaws so embrace this knowledge with gusto and let's go for it! Here are some tips that will help you bring out the best in yourself.

- **If you're petite and want to appear taller, purchase suits or suit separates with vertical pin or chalk stripes.** Consider three-button jackets in solids or pin-striped. Avoid plaid, tweed and double-breasted jackets, which add width rather than height. You want to have a continuing vertical line from head to toe, so consider wearing a monochromatic color scheme in your clothing ensemble. Consider ribbed sweaters and shirts with vertical stripes. Pants should be hemmed to create only a slight break in the trouser as the pant front rests on the shoe. Avoid cuffed trousers.

- **If you want to minimize your height, emphasize horizontal lines.** Try plaid patterns and double-breasted jackets. Consider a jacket or top in one color and the trousers in another. Choose cuffed pants as well. Wear shirts, tops and sweaters that have horizontal lines in the pattern.

- **If you're heavy, choose dark colors such as black, navy, and dark gray.** Also incorporate pin-stripes in the pants and shirts. Double-breasted jackets can be slimming if the buttons are closely spaced. Avoid bulky sweaters and choose trim ones with set-in sleeves and minimal texture. Avoid horizontal lines and extra details as those found in cargo pants. As well, avoid decorative fabrics that are highly patterned, such as camouflage, or shiny, or those that add extra weight such corduroy. Wear plain front pants with minimal structural or decorative designs and make sure that they fit around your waist. Avoid hip huggers.

- **If you want to appear heavier, consider tweeds, glen plaids, and madras plaids as well as wool flannel, linen, cotton and corduroy.** Introduce pleated pants, bulky tops, and use warm bright colors and white. Consider European-cut and double-vented jackets and suits. Avoid fabrics that cling in tops and shirts. Emphasize horizontal stripes in sweaters and shirts.

- **If your shoulders are wider than your hips, consider double-pleated pants to add balance to your bottom half.** Consider wearing pants that are lighter in color than your shirts, such as a denim shirt with khaki twills. Avoid epaulets and other details at the shoulders, and consider jackets with patch pockets to add width to your lower half and balance your body.

- **If your hips are the same or wider than your shoulders, emphasize the shoulders and chest and minimize the lower half.** Choose bulky sweaters, tweed sport coats and boxed-styled jackets, such as jean or bomber jacket styles. Wear lighter colors on top and darker ones on the bottom, such as dark-gray flannel trousers and a light-colored cardigan and button-down pinpoint oxford or denim shirt. Wear plain-front pants without cuffs with minimal detail.
- **If your legs are short, avoid cuffed pants.** Consider pants that have vertical stripes such as pin or chalked striped or corduroy. Three button jackets also add length.
- **If your shoulders are extremely sloped, choose jackets with padding.** Avoid raglan sleeves in sweaters and shirts since they only emphasize the slope. Choose set-in sleeves and jacket lapels that point upward. Avoid unstructured jackets at all costs.
- **If your shoulders are square, do wear raglan sleeves but avoid extremes in lapel-width such as very wide and very narrow.** Choose unstructured jackets with natural shoulders.
- **As we age, most men will gain weight in their stomach and loose much of their derriere. To combat this, make sure that pants fit around the waist and not below.** In most circumstances, the pants will need to be taken in at the rear. When choosing pants or jeans, make sure they fit and consider those with back pocket detail such as flap pockets to add weight to this area.

Slimming Secrets for Men and Women

If you want to appear about 10 pounds lighter, the clothing you wear can help you do that. Consider these tips to minimizing your size.

- **Black or dark colors slenderize any area.** If you're bottom heavy, wear a dark color on the bottom and a light or bright shirt on top. The bright color or pattern draws the eye upward to your face.
- **Avoid shiny or heavily textured fabrics.** Shiny fabrics make

any area appear larger because they reflect light. Heavily textured fabrics only add extra weight.

- **Incorporate vertical lines, either decoratively in the fabric pattern or structurally as in vertical darts, princess seams, or a placket down the front.** Also consider incorporating long chains or scarves around the neck. As well, consider three-quarter length sleeves or roll up long sleeves once or twice. When wearing a jacket, put the collar up.

- **Avoid tight-fitting clothing, since it only emphasizes your weight gain and draws attention to the extra pounds.** At the same time, recognize that covering up your weight gain will not solve your problem since it just promotes unnecessary weight.

- **Introduce simple angular lines, such as A-line skirts, tailor-notched collar shirts and blouses, and tailored jackets.** These lines offset the roundness of the body and bring it into balance. Plain front pants and skirts are recommended over pleated varieties.

- **Minimize the use of horizontal lines, as in belts, cuffed pants and border print skirts, as they add extra width to your body frame.**

- **If you have large legs, try dark hose such as black tights or socks or sheer hose in charcoal or dark gray or coffee.** Make sure that if you wear a skirt that the hemline does not fall at the widest point of the calf. Instead, wear a skirt that falls at the knee and wear heels as opposed to flats to add length.

Conclusion

Part of being human is acknowledging that we're not perfect. Given that everyone has a figure flaw of one kind or another, we can address them with simple tricks such as those presented in this chapter. Embrace your individuality and wear clothing that helps you put your best foot forward. You are an asset – maximize it!

10

Create Impact with Accessories

Nothing individualizes a look or pulls everything together better than accessories. It's probably one of the most important components of dressing, whether for work or after. Even so, it's often the least considered. We may not be able to buy a new outfit every month or season. However, we can certainly afford to update our look through accessories. In fact, when the economy takes a nose dive, as in the "Great Recession," department stores increase square footage allocated to accessories because people still want to buy – just not that much.

Both men and women have lots of accessories to consider that add miles to any wardrobe. If you have very few pieces devoted to your work apparel, accessories can add miles. For example, I went for two and a half months to Romania to teach. Because of baggage restrictions, I only was able to carry about six tops and two pairs of pants for the entire time. But where I put the emphasis was on scarves, belts and jewelry to change up the look.

Accessories also serve the important role of drawing attention to your face. By using accessories strategically, you can showcase your best features. As well, accessories include your carrying case for your laptop or tablet computer, since it is part of what you carry. You'll want to consider such purchases carefully since we're tending to never be without access to the Internet and our files!

Accessories provide the finishing touches and individualize your look. So with that in mind, let's take a closer look at how you can use accessories to complete your outfit.

For Women

Women have such a variety of accessories to choose from that each day can be a something new even with a limited wardrobe. From jewelry to belts and shoes to scarves and shawls women have a multitude of ways to change up an outfit and never get bored.

Scarves

A scarf is one of the easiest accessories to work with. They serve the purpose of adding color and interest, as well as providing comfort from air-conditioned offices or cool outdoor temperatures. Scarves come in a wide variety of shapes and sizes, and they can be worn so many ways. You can find them in a variety of fabrics, such as silk, chenille, rayon, cotton and wool, and they can be thick or translucent. Consider building an assortment of scarves to wear around the neck, shoulders or waist, and you'll be prepared to add excitement to your outfits.

Here are some ideas for using scarves for impact:

- **Small squares can be folded and tied around the neck.** If your neck is short, avoid this approach. However, do it if your neck is long.
- **A medium square can be folded over into a triangle and worn campfire style.** Or turn it to the side for interest over the shoulder or with the triangle in front.
- **Large square scarves can also be folded to create a triangle and worn around the shoulders.** They can folded into a rectangle and worn over the shoulder with a belt. Wear a scarf tied as an ascot worn at the neck with an open collared shirt.
- **An oblong scarf is perfect folded and wrapped around the neck with the ends hanging in the front.**
- **Consider silk pocket-squares or small squares for the breast pocket of your jacket.** They can be worn either with the ends pointed out or tucked in. Pocket squares are commonly found in the men's accessory departments in clothing stores and are smaller in size than small squares found in women's accessory departments.

There are plenty of websites that can provide additional information on the different types of scarves and how to tie them. Here's one in particular to check out: www.greatestlook.com.

Hosiery

Hosiery comes in a variety of designs, colors and sizes. They can be opaque as in tights or very sheer. Avoid the fishnets and those with a seam down the back. However, consider those with vertical stripes either worn with skirts or trousers. Also, utilize knee-highs for trousers and long skirts.

If you want to wear color, pick one that matches the color of the skirt, trouser or shoe. Black opaque tights are acceptable for work; however, also consider sheers in colors for a more sophisticated classic look. Avoid red and multicolored hosiery, period. If your legs are heavy, avoid calling attention to them with hosiery that has designs or color.

Belts

Belts offer lots of possibilities for pulling a look together. Also, there is so much variety to choose from, including chains, leather and fabric. Belt in an oversized shirt or jacket. Try a different belt than the one that came with the garment. You might even consider eliminating the threaded belt loops on the side seams altogether so you can interchange belts easily.

Consider the width and texture of the belt and your body type. For example, if you have a large waist, avoid cinching it in but rather wear a narrow belt loosely over a shirt.

Think about using belts at the waist, above it to create an empire look, or below the waist for variety. Besides belting trousers and jeans, try belting a skirt, particularly if it has an elasticized waist. Think about getting a double wrap belt that is great over shirts and tunics.

Here are a couple more tips for using belts:

- **Belt a cardigan over a top for one look or just belt the top and wear the cardigan over it.**
- **If you choose to buy a belt with gold or silver metal buckles, make sure that you match up your jewelry to the metal in the belt.**

Jewelry

Jewelry makes a strong impact with any outfit. However, be cautious not to overdo it. Rings on every finger, tons of bracelets, and five pairs of earrings are *too much*. Consider starting out with basics, such as gold, silver and pearls, in short and long chains and earrings. Don't forget pendants and broaches. They add interest to jackets, simple blouses, scarves and cardigans. Then start adding to your collection with interesting pieces with stones and other designs in a variety of metals. You can take a simple outfit such as a denim shirt and trousers, put on a great turquoise necklace and earrings, and you're done. An interesting or dramatic piece around the neck, along with earrings, is all you need to wear with a black cocktail dress for an evening out.

When it comes to earrings, consider hoops, buttons or dangling styles. Try to keep them to one per ear, and if you have an interesting pair, let those be the focus. Don't take away from their interest with a competing necklace. Just wear a simple necklace or belt to add impact. If you're a winter or summer (regarding your skin tone), consider silver rather than gold, while springs and autumns look best with gold. Moreover, make sure that the jewelry is in proportion to your size. If you're large, you are fortunate to be able to wear big pieces of jewelry. Meanwhile, the same would swallow a petite or small individual. Keep this in mind when you see something that you'd like to add to your jewelry assortment. Also, consider the weight of necklaces and what it might feel like at the end of the day. Keep the pieces light in weight, especially if you have neck problems.

Handbags & Carrying Cases

When it comes to handbags, have one that goes with the majority of your work wardrobe. You might change it up for warmer versus cool months. However, you don't want to be spending time transferring your things from one bag to another. Consider a "bag in a bag" or a purse organizer from www.purseperfector.com. This product makes easy to change bags and leave nothing behind.

Further, make sure that the bag is in proportion to *your* size. Although big bags are in fashion, consider one that is a bit smaller if you're petite; otherwise it will overwhelm you. If you have large hips, avoid shoulder bags that land at the hips; they will only adds extra weight at the widest point. Avoid loud colors, such as fire engine red. Rather, choose your bag in a wardrobe neutral, such as black, brown or navy.

When it comes to a brief case or something for carrying your laptop, give some thought to what will work best for you. Nylon styles are rugged and lightweight; however, they may not be appealing in style. If you travel extensively, check out the Transportation Security Agency's website (www.tsa.gov) for guidelines for a good laptop bag that can get through security easily. Give as much consideration to what you'll be carrying your papers and laptop in as well as your handbag. As well, if you have a tablet computer, you'll want an appropriate cover to protect it and to communicate your professionalism and individual style.

Shoes

An important accessory, shoes get us from one place to another by foot. Although platforms and high, high heels are in fashion and celebrities wear them, realize that the stars have them on for just the red carpet and photo shoot and then they change their footware. Consider simple styles that are comfortable and interchangeable; however, avoid skimmers, sandals and flip-flops. Pumps and loafer styles are great, and they go with pants, jeans, dresses and skirts. Boots are a great option, and these can be worn with jeans either in or out. Consider footware by Munro, Trotters, Cole Hahn and other brands that focus on comfort as well as looks.

In choosing the colors of your shoes, avoid those that can be worn with only one outfit, such as red. Consider focusing on wardrobe neutral hues, like black, taupe, navy and brown. Keep design to a minimum since you don't want people staring at your feet when they should be looking at the total you. Avoid white shoes, unless you're in the nursing profession, and try beige or light camel. If you have large feet, white will only make them appear larger, and that'll be the first thing that people see when they look at you. As well, save the gold and silver shoes for "after five" formal occasions; yet, do consider bronze and other darker metallic leather styles for work.

Glasses

This is an accessory which can glamorize your look while helping you to see. Frames should softly follow the shape of the face, without emphasizing facial contour. If your face is round, round glasses will only accentuate it. Make sure that the frames you choose do not go too far down your cheeks, for then they'll look too big. If you want shaded lenses, go with a 5 to 10 percent tint in the same color as your eyes. Transition lenses are great for avoiding the change into sunglasses when going outdoors, so consider these as well.

If you wear readers, consider multiple pairs – such as one pair at the office, one in your bag, and several at home (depending on where you spend your time). Give these the same consideration as regular glasses. You may need bifocals or trifocals, and if so, you'll need to decide whether to go with one with lines or a transition; there are trade-offs to both. The choice is yours.

Another pair of glasses that you may want to consider are ones for working on the computer. These often come in orange tint and help to reflect the light waves from the computer screen; you'll find them at CVS or other major retailers. You may also want to check with your eye-care professional regarding those that can be special-ordered for your prescription.

Undergarments

Here's an accessory that you don't see but which completes an outfit. Today women have lots of options regarding control and shape so let's get started.

If you are full or large busted, purchase *bras* that provide plenty of support such as underwire varieties with thicker straps. You may also choose minimizer bras that minimize the largeness of the breasts. If you're small busted, consider padded or Wonderbra types to give you that added shape. No matter what your size, provide support for the breast tissue – especially when exercising.

When considering the purchase of undergarments give a lot attention to fit. This is particularly true for bras. To determine your cup size, measure yourself with a tape measure first around the rib cage right underneath the breasts, then around the middle of the breasts across the nipple. The difference between these two measurements will determine your cup size:

- A one-inch difference is a size A.
- Two inches is a size B.

- Three inches is size C.
- Four inches is a D.
- A five-inch difference is an E.

Check to make sure that the middle of the front of the bra lies comfortably on the sternum bone. The bra should fasten comfortably on the middle hooks. Finally, purchase bras with cups that are seamless so that they don't show through your shirt, sweater or blouse. Your bra should hold your breasts in place and conceal your nipples.

Wear *panties* that fit appropriately, do not create indentions, and don't show through in pants and skirts. If they start riding up, you need a larger size. Use color with caution, making sure your panties won't be seen through your clothes. This is particularly true when wearing white and beige pants and skirts or thin fabrics. If wearing a translucent blouse, wear a camisole underneath to camouflage your bra.

When it comes to body shaping and slimming, *Spanx* is a wonderful discovery. Girdles inhibit circulation; however, Spanx products are lighter and provide some shape and smoothing. The Spanx brand is available in panties, slips and body suit varieties.

Choose your undergarments in neutral skin tones, such as brown or beige. Avoid white since it shows through. If you want to wear dark undergarments, wear dark tops and bottoms.

Hats

Once common, women's hats are not acceptable for the workplace whether it's an Easter bonnet or a baseball cap. As well, refrain from scarves tied around the head for work.

For Men

Accessories for men are growing as well as what they can do with the same pieces is also evolving. For years the focus was just on men's ties; however, with scarves, jewelry, hosiery, belts and bags, men have a multitude of options to change up the same outfit.

Hosiery

There's lot of variety in men's hosiery. Choose from solids or patterned; however, avoid white socks and opt for those that closely match the color of your shoes or the color of your trousers. Avoid the bright argyles and go for subtle patterns so as to not present a distraction. As well, get socks that stay up on your legs. When the legs are crossed, as in sitting, the leg is exposed, so make sure your socks go over the calf.

Belts

This is another accessory that comes in a wide variety for men, from fabric and rope to leather. If suits are required, go with a leather belt with a conservative belt buckle; choose either brown, cordovan or black leather. You'll want the belt to match the shoes.

If jackets are optional and jeans are permitted, your options expand. Consider braided leather, military styles, and stretch varieties. With cargo pants and jeans, think about military styles. If wearing twills, go with traditional styles or braided leather. Stretch with leather closings is also great for twills, and they provide comfort.

When considering colors, avoid white and opt for beige, navy and olive, or with leather, choose brown and cordovan. Black is normally worn for formal occasions. Bottom line: If your pants have belt loops and you're tucking your shirt in, wear a belt. As well, belts help keep the pants at the waist so it's important to wear them. The belt should close on the third or fourth hole, and the width should be a minimum of an inch wide up to an inch and a half when it comes to choosing styles for work.

Suspenders are an option if you don't want to wear a belt, but don't wear both. Many trousers are equipped with buttons on the inside of the waist so that suspenders can be attached. Avoid the kind of suspenders that clip on.

Jewelry

Jewelry, such as watches, bracelets, tie chains and earrings, have become common for men. If you do wear earrings, keep them small and limited to one pair so as to not distract from your face. Lapel pins and class rings are an option to accessorize with jewelry; however, avoid excessive amounts of these accessories, such as a large gold or silver chains and bracelets.

If you choose to wear a watch, consider a sport or classic tailored style. Find one that is a minimum of 40 mm or one and a half inches in size, clearly tells the time, but is not a show piece.

Cufflinks for shirts are often a choice for those who work where suits are required. You'll want to keep these jeweled accessories classically styled and simple, so consider gold, silver or stone varieties.

Glasses

Eyeglasses can add to or detract from your appearance. Frames should pick up the color from your hair. Consider frames in silver, black or frameless. Heavier-built men can wear heavier frames. In choosing frames, select a style that compliments your facial contour. For example, if you have a round face, consider angular shape frames.

If you want shaded lenses, go with a 5 to 10 percent tint in the same color as your eyes. Transition lenses are a great way to avoid having to change into sunglasses but realize that they take time to switch from light to dark and vice versa.

If you wear readers, consider several pairs for accessibility. Give these the same consideration as regular glasses. As you age you might need bifocals or trifocals so consider the various options to address this decision such as those with lines and transition styles. Both have plusses and minuses depending on what is important to you.

As I mentioned earlier, if you work on the computer extensively you may consider glasses that help reflect the harmful rays that are emitted. Some stores now carry frames with orange tinted lenses for computers users so consider these to protect your eyes.

Scarves

Over the last few years, scarves have become a major accessory for men. In the past, men have mostly worn a pocket square or silk kerchief in the breast pocket of their jackets. Now scarves are acceptable to wear, and they're no longer confined to around the neck for warmth with an overcoat. Long scarves in medium to lightweight fabrics complete the look of a T-shirt, jeans and a jacket. Consider the Parisian knot or wearing one loose around the neck and knotted. Whatever you decide, make sure that the scarf coordinates with what you're wearing.

Scarves can be worn with pullover tops and with shirts instead of ties, depending on the nature of your business. Consider folding a large square into a triangle and tying the ends at the back of the neck with the triangle draped in front.

Go to http://www.askmen.com/fashion/fashiontip_300/357_fashion_ advice.html for more information on selecting and tying scarves.

Bags & Cases

Popular in Europe and frankly quite handy are "man bags." Rather than sit on your wallet, consider a tailored man bag in leather. Some varieties have shoulder straps, while others do not. The choice is yours. Another alternative to wallets and bags look like small notebooks; they hold credit cards and can fit in the pocket inside your sport coat or blazer.

Other "bags" to include as important accessories are briefcases or laptop carrying cases. If you travel extensively, go to the Transportation Security Administration website, www.tsa.gov, to learn about laptop carrying cases that go through security easily. Consider a case that reflects your professionalism and personality, if you need to have one. As well in this day of technology, you'll want a case for your tablet computer that is appropriate for your work style and who you are.

Shoes

Types of men's shoes include a wide variety of tie and slip-ons, depending on your workplace requirements. If suits are required, consider tailored styles such as wing tipped, oxford or tie styles. As well, consider loafers and slip-ons. Avoid boat or deck shoes and sneakers.

If jackets are optional or jeans are permitted, classic loafers, either with a flap and/or tassel or without, are great choices. Stay away from sandals and soft leather shoes, but do consider boat/deck shoes. No flip-flops.

If you work construction, consider work boots such as the brand Red Wing that have a metal tip to protect your toes.

Undergarments

Although undergarments are not worn outside, they do help complete a look, and they are essential. Underwear and t-shirts have come a long way from white and boxers or briefs. The bottom line: Be conscious of what you're wearing underneath, as well as what you show to others. For example, if you're wearing a dress shirt, wear an *undershirt or t-shirt* with it. Consider a V-neck style so the collar of the t-shirt does not show through when the shirt is open.

Regarding *underwear*, you have a choice of hipsters, bikini, regular and long briefs, and boxers in lots of colors besides white. With boxers, you have choices too with tapered and regular. (Tapered boxers are cut slimmer in the leg than regular boxers.) Choose a style that is comfortable for you; if you choose bikini or hipster styles, make sure that the lines don't show through your pants. As well, if you choose colored briefs, make sure that the color doesn't show through. Although with many young people, the fashion is to show your underwear, that's not appropriate for work – no matter what you do.

Additionally, men have options regarding body shaping and smoothing. For those that wear T-shirts or thin pullovers, consider a lightweight *Spanx* brand smoother so your breast nipples don't show through. However, if you want to minimize those five pounds you gained over the holidays, Spanx has stronger body smoothers available. Just don't expect them to take your waist from a 45 to a 38.

Conclusion

We all get bored with what is in our closet and want something new. By investing in the variety of accessories that are available for men and women you can basically have a new look each and every day. Moreover, accessories complete the look of any wardrobe ensemble and give it pizzazz! Now you don't have any excused for being bored!

11

Take Care of Your Investment

Clothes are not meant to last. However, if you don't take care of them, they will really perish before their time. It won't seem like long before the hem comes out of a pair of trousers or a button falls off a shirt. Moreover, knowing what you're getting regarding care requirements helps you to make better purchases. Taking care of your clothes, including your shoes, will save money in the long run and give you truly a working wardrobe. If you're not one to replace a button, your neighborhood dry cleaners may be able to save the day. They can also launder and press your shirts and make minor alterations.

Hangers

Caring for your wardrobe starts with the hangers. Invest in plastic, wood or padded fabric hangers. For the majority of your clothing, the plastic hangers will be perfect. For heavier items, such as blazers, consider wood hangars; however, the plastic ones will suffice. For knits, leather and delicates, consider the padded hangers. The problem with wire hangers is that they can rust and stain your clothing. Especially if you live in a humid climate, such as Miami, Arkansas or Bangkok, the metal hangers will definitely rust; so go with plastic to hang your clothes.

Storing Clothing

When you pick up your dry cleaning, take off the plastic wrap before you hang the clothes in the closet. They need to air out. When storing your clothes for some time, purchase garment bags made of natural fabrics that breathe rather than the plastic ones. This will save the clothes from any mildew stains. Also make sure that your clothes are free from stains prior to storing. Fruit stains fade garments over time, and any type of food stain attracts moths. As an alternative to mothballs, consider cedar chips that are a natural deterrent against moths. When storing wool items, place them in a dry area free from sunlight, and consider placing them in garment bags with cedar siding to prevent damage from insects.

Caring for Fabrics

Most items today can be machine washed and dried. Washing machines have a multitude of settings that accommodate delicate as well as sturdy fabrics. Understand that the principle behind washers getting your items cleaned is through rubbing garments together; so make sure that you don't overload the machine when doing the wash. Also, get acquainted with all the settings and the fabrics that are possible to wash. This way, you'll get optimal cleaning results. Finally, make sure that your machine remains rust free by letting it air dry once you have finished using it.

As well, dryers today are capable of handling more types of fabrics than in the past. Again, review the manufacturer's instructions and settings. Keep the dryer in peak performance by removing lint from the lint drawer each time, and check that there is no build-up of lint behind the dryer. If you have a tendency to use fabric softening sheets in each load, try reusing them; this helps reduce build-up in the dryer.

If items must be professionally cleaned, ask friends which dry cleaner they recommend. A good dry cleaner changes their cleaning fluid frequently and steams without heating the garment to an extreme degree. When picking up your dry cleaning, there shouldn't be an odor to the clothes. If there is, that's a clear sign that the cleaner doesn't change their fluid regularly enough. Traditional dry cleaners use a solvent called perchloroethylene that is effective in cleaning; however, for less toxic dry cleaning methods consider those companies that use liquid silicone, liquefied carbon dioxide, or biodegradable detergents as their cleaning agent.

Wool

This is fabulous fabric that keeps you warm in the winter and cool in the summer. However, to have your wool items last the life that they should care for them appropriately. For instance, after each wearing of a wool jacket, take things out of your pockets, any pins off the lapels, and brush the item lightly. Let the garment air out at least 24 hours before wearing it again.

Do not wash your washable wool items after each wearing; this will destroy the fibers. If you do need to wash one of these pieces, check the care label for directions. Otherwise, most machine washers, on the delicate cycle, can handle wool clothing. Never put wool in the dryer, rather air dry it on a flat surface. Wool only needs to be dry cleaned once a season.

Steam rather than press your wool items to release the wrinkles. If your wool item gets a hole, take it to a professional who can reweave the wool fabric. If you have the extra thread that came with the garment when you purchased it, bring it along. Otherwise, they can use the extra fabric found in the seam allowance.

Cotton

Most cotton items can be washed easily in the washing machine. Separate your light- weight cottons (such as t-shirts and tops) from heavier ones (such as jeans and sweatshirts). Combine like colors together. Use a regular laundry detergent, and if needed, pre-treat stains prior to washing. Do not apply bleach or all fabric bleach direct to the fabric; not only will this remove the color, it will weaken the fibers. If the cotton items are delicate, use the gentle or hand-wash cycle on the machine. Otherwise, use the normal cycle with cool or warm water. Dry on high or medium heat. Press items with a hot iron, preferably on the cotton setting.

Silk

A beautiful fabric, silk has a lovely drape, is strong, and absorbs dyes easily. Most silk must be dry cleaned or hand-washed unless it is prewashed silk. Prewashed silk is machine washable, using cool or cold water on the hand wash or gentle cycle. Further, only prewashed silk can be tumble dried in the dryer on the low heat setting. Other silk garments can be hand-washed with mild liquid soap and dried flat. When pressing silk, use the delicate setting on your iron.

Synthetics

These fabrics include as polyester, acrylic, Lycra spandex, acetate, nylon, olefin or cotton with a permanent press finish. They are easy to care for and look good; however, they have special concerns. For example, synthetics are heat sensitive and pick up oil-based stains easily. Because they are heat sensitive, avoid putting synthetics in the dryer on a high or hot setting. The fabrics will soften and form permanent wrinkles that cannot be fixed. Rather use the low heat or the knit setting for synthetics, and remove them promptly to hang up when the cycle is completed. As well, to avoid permanent wrinkles created in the wash, do not overload the washer and avoid hot temperatures. Cool or cold temperatures are fine for synthetics. Further, do not use chlorine bleach. A moderate temperature on the iron is all that is necessary to press synthetics.

Synthetics love oil; so if they get an oil-based stain, they'll need extra care to get it out. When the stain happens, blot it immediately, but don't rub. Then rub salt into the stain. Then, at home, use a prewash and soak the item. Be sure that the stain is out before drying the item, since drying sets the stain. As a side note with acetate, the acetone found in nail polish remover will dissolve the fabric; so be cautious when around acetone-based products.

Rayon

This is a regenerated cellulosic fiber made from dissolving bleached wood pulp. Since there are a lot of solvents and solutions involved with creating this fabric, avoid it if you have sensitive skin. The fabric, also known as the brand Tencel, accepts dyes easily but needs special care. When hand-washing the fabric, avoid using Woolite but rather pick a mild liquid soap or detergent. Do not use stain removers since they will fade the color. If you machine wash a rayon item, use a cool or cold temperature and the gentle cycle. If the item is stained with an oil-based stain, put liquid dish soap on the stain, then put the clothes in the washer. Tumble dry on medium or low heat, and remove promptly. Use the steam setting when ironing, and consider ironing the item on the wrong side to protect the fabric from damage to the outside.

Hemp

Hemp is one of the few fabrics that gets stronger when wet. Garments made of hemp can be machine washed and tumble dried in the dryer.

Ramie

A baste fiber (a plant fiber taken from the skin of stems), ramie is much like cotton, linen and jute. Ramie has also been called "China Grass," and it has been cultivated in Asia for hundreds of years. It's now also grown in Egypt, France, Italy, Indonesia and Russia! As a natural cellulosic fiber, Ramie looks much like linen and can be coarse like canvas. The best way to take care of this fiber is to have it professionally dry cleaned; however, if blended with synthetics, ramie can be machine washed. When pressing garments made of Ramie, use the cotton or linen setting on your iron.

Leather Shoes, Garments & Bags

Shoe care is simple but extremely important. Shoes are expensive, especially well-made leather ones. No matter what grade of leather shoes you own, take care of them and polish them with a cream rather than liquid polish. Polish protects the leather from drying out or being ruined by a sudden rain. If you do get caught in the rain, let your shoes dry naturally away from such direct heat as a radiator. Stuff the toe area with paper towels to absorb moisture and to help retain the shape of the shoe. Remove any salt or stains with white vinegar and water mixed in equal parts. Once they have dried out, condition and polish the shoes.

At the end of the day, take your shoes off and let them air out for 24 hours. Consider using a shoe tree to keep your finer shoes in shape. Also, put your shoes in clear shoe boxes; this will help keep the dirt and dust from the air off of them. In cold climates, the salt on the roads and sidewalks should be removed from your leather items immediately with a soft cloth and warm water. Leave the items in a dry cool place.

Check the soles and heels of your shoes periodically. Are they worn out, with holes? Send them to your local cobbler immediately. Give the same consideration to your other leather goods, such as brief cases and bags. When you purchase a new leather brief case, treat it to a paste-polish rub down to keep soil from penetrating.

With new leather garments, such as pants, jackets and vests, treat them with a leather protector spray before wearing. Further, keep the garments dry when wearing and hang them on broad, padded hangers. Regarding liquid stains, blot the stain immediately to remove the excess amount. However, ink, paint, colognes, perfumes, hairspray and chemical stains can't be removed, so avoid these when wearing leather. For powder, dust or mud, use a damp sponge with warm water and wipe clean. With suede items, brush lightly away any dust or dirt after wearing.

Care Instructions

US law mandates that care instructions be attached to all apparel; so if you don't have any idea how to care for an item, follow the manufacturers' suggested instructions. But what do these instructions mean? First, if the temperature is not mentioned, then any will do. Cold water saves colors, and it is just as effective as hot when cleaning clothes. However, if you have allergies or asthma, use hot water for bedding and some apparel – such as jeans – to kill dust mites and other allergens. If bleach is not mentioned, than any bleach may be used; however, with colors, use a color-safe bleach such as Clorox 2. To boost the effectiveness of your detergent, consider adding white vinegar or baking soda in the wash cycle. Also, white vinegar is effective in keeping colors from transferring to others in the wash.

If ironing instructions are not mentioned, that means the fabric is treated or constructed in such a way that ironing is not necessary. However, you may find that it may still need to be pressed; if so, use a temperature that is appropriate for the fabric. If it's a synthetic, use a low temperature since the linen or cotton setting will probably melt the fabric.

Given the variety of instructions put out by manufacturers, I decided to provide the more common ones and their interpretations*:

- **Machine Wash**: Use an automatic washer.
- **Warm**: Initial water temperature setting 90 F to 110 F (32 to 43 C). The temperature should be comfortable to the hands.
- **Cold**: Initial water temperature setting same as cold tap water up to 85 F (29 C).
- **Do Not Have Commercially Laundered**: Don't employ a

laundry that uses special formulations, sour rinses, or extremely high temperatures, or one that is employed for commercial, industrial or institutional purposes since these methods may destroy the fabric.

- **Small Load**: Use a smaller than normal wash load.
- **Delicate Cycle or Gentle Cycle**: Set washer to gentle cycle with slow agitation and reduced time.
- **Durable Press Cycle or Permanent Press Cycle**: Suggested because it uses a cool-down rinse or cold rinse before spinning.
- **Separately**: Wash alone.
- **With Like Colors**: Wash with garments that are similar in color and brightness. For example, you might wash a load of dark colors and then a load of light colors to ensure minimal color transfer.
- **Wash Inside Out**: To protect the surface of the garment, turn it inside out. This is also effective if there are epaulets and other details that might be damaged from the abrasion that occurs in the wash cycle.
- **Warm Rinse**: Initial water temperature setting should be 90 to 110 F (32 to 43 C).
- **Cold Rinse**: Initial water temperature setting should be like cold tap water.
- **Rinse Thoroughly**: Rinse several times to remove soap, bleach, detergent or color that is not set in. This is common with fabrics with rich colors such as those from India and Indonesia.
- **No Spin or Do Not Spin**: Remove material at the start of the final spin cycle.
- **No Wring or Do Not Wring**: Do not wring by hand and don't use a roller wringer.
- **Hand Wash**: Use water, detergent, or soap and gently squeeze the garment several times.
- **Damp Wipe Only**: Clean fabric surface with a damp cloth or sponge.
- **Tumble Dry**: Use machine dryer.
- **Medium**: Use medium heat setting on the dryer.
- **Low**: Use low heat setting on the dryer.

- **Durable Press or Permanent Press**: Use permanent press setting on the dryer.
- **No Heat**: Use the air dry selection on the dryer.
- **Remove Promptly**: When items are dry, remove them from the dryer to avoid wrinkling.
- **Drip Dry**: Air dry, without wringing or shaping, on a plastic or padded hanger.
- **Iron**: Ironing is needed. Any temperature is safe.
- **Warm Iron**: Set the iron at a medium temperature.
- **Cool Iron**: Set the iron at the lowest temperature.
- **Do Not Iron**: This is for garments that don't need to be smoothed or finished with an iron.
- **No Steam or Do Not Steam**: Refrain from using steam when ironing.
- **Iron Wrong Side Only**: Turn item inside out when ironing.
- **Steam Only**: Steam with steamer or iron with steam but use no contact pressure.
- **Use a Press Cloth**: Use a dry iron or a damp cloth between the iron and the garment when ironing.
- **Bleach When Needed**: Any bleach can be used when necessary.
- **No Bleach or Do Not Bleach**: Self-explanatory.
- **Wash or Dry Clean, Any Normal Method**: Can be machine washed, dried and ironed at any temperature. Any bleach can be used. Garment can be dry cleaned using any kind of solvent.
- **Dry Clean**: Can be dry cleaned at a professional or self-service dry cleaners or at home. (Involves a process whereby soil is removed by organic solvents in a machine).
- **Professionally Dry Clean**: Use a professional dry cleaner; avoid self-service or home dry cleaning.

*This care guide courtesy of the Consumer Affairs Committee, American Apparel Manufacturers Association, and based on the Voluntary Guide of the Textile Industry Advisory Committee for Consumer Interest. For more information go to http://www.textileaffairs. com/lguide.htm

Removing Stains

It's inevitable that we will spill something or just end up with a clothes stain without knowing how it got there. Getting rid of stains is an art but it can save tons of money if you can prevent your clothes from being ruined. Bottom line: When you get a stain, act quickly. Don't complete the cleaning cycle until you know the stain is out. Drying heat sets a stain. If you're prone to spilling things on your clothes, you might consider carrying a Tide To-Go cleaning stick; these sticks are available in packages of three at your grocery store. The sticks are great for most fabric stains when they happen. As with any spot remover, test the fabric in a hidden area first to make sure the stick doesn't fade or harm it.

Here are some more tips to help you deal with removing stains.

- **Pencil**: Use a prewash stain remover on the stain; allow it to set in and then wash the clothes.
- **Ink**: If you get an ink stain, apply hairspray or rubbing alcohol to it. Use paper towels to absorb the stain. Then wash in warm water. Do not dry in the dryer until the stain is completely gone since the heat sets the stain.
- **Ketchup**: Blot the excess ketchup, and then rinse the stained area in cool water mixed with mild detergent. Use a prewash spot remover and then run the clothes through the wash cycle. Let it air dry and check to see if the stain is gone. If not, go through the steps again.
- **Gum**: Put the garment in the freezer for about 6 hours and then chip the gum off. Or apply ice cubes to harden the gum so it can be easily removed.
- **Protein-Based Stains**: Examples include blood, cheese sauce, gelatin, baby formula and milk. Soak and agitate clothes stained by these items in cold water before washing.
- **Tannin Stains**: Examples include alcoholic drinks, beer, coffee, cologne, berries, tea and soft drinks. Use detergent, not bar soap, in the hottest water possible for the fabric and soak the item before running it through the wash cycle.
- **Oil-Based Stains**: Examples include automotive oil, salad dressings, mayonnaise, face cream, and body lotions. Pre-treat

these stains with a heavy duty detergent applied to the stain or apply a powder detergent paste to the stain before washing.

- **Dye Stains**: Examples include Kool-Aid, grass, cherries and blueberries. Pre-treat these stains with a heavy duty detergent or soak the item in a diluted solution of all-fabric power bleach for a maximum of 15 minutes. (More information is available at http://ohioline.osu.edu/outside/stainrem.html)

- **Deodorant and Perspiration Stains**: These are those yellow stains under the arms in shirts and blouses, and they're the result of the deodorant formula still being wet when the garment is put on as well as the aluminum salts found in antiperspirants. To remove these stains, soak shirts in warm water with an enzyme presoak or rub the area with white vinegar. After that, wash the item in the hottest temperature possible that is safe for the fabric. If the stain remains, dampen it and sprinkle with meat tenderizer and let it stand for an hour. Then wash.

Conclusion

Caring for what you wear will ensure that your clothing looks its best for years to come. In this day and time, clothing is a major investment – especially when it comes to what we wear for work. Take care of your clothes and they will take care of you.

12

Skin Deep

The skin is the largest organ of the body, yet most people give it the least consideration. Only until the signs of aging start to appear in our 30s and 40s, do we give it more thought. This is not just about the face but our entire body. There are important considerations, not only for work but for our well-being. Taking care of our skin is essential to a professional look for both men and women. The world envies youth so looking vibrant is a plus in the workplace. For men and women, taking care of the skin is the first step in holding off our "age" as we mature. You want to be a seasoned professional, not an old one.

In this chapter I will outline the steps for a basic skin care regimen for men and women with additional tips for men since they shave. You may be surprised that taking care of your skin really doesn't involve a lot of time, work or expense. As well, I will share remedies for some skin problems that are experienced by many and that increase with age such as adult acne and hyperpigmentation. Finally, I will address taking care of other areas of our body so that we can become "comfortable in our own skin!"

Basic Skin Care

It doesn't matter how young or old you are, it's critical to take care of your skin. Although we can't change genetics and its effect on our skin, we can minimize the damage of environmental factors on our face and body. One of the worst culprits in premature aging is the sun. I'm sure you've heard a lot about the increase in skin cancer. Bottom line: The sun is not our friend. Whether you're one year old, 20, 55 or older, it's essential to protect your skin from the sun and ultraviolet exposure of any kind (including tanning beds). You may not see it now but guaranteed you WILL see the damage from the sun later – in the form of freckles that don't go away, sun or liver spots, wrinkles, and leather-like skin. If you have an office window, drive a lot, or bike to work, you will get exposed to damaging rays. Wearing sunscreen is a start but may I suggest SUN BLOCK, on a level of at least SPF 50. It's stronger and provides more protection than sun screen. In addition to sun block, may I suggest a hat with a wide brim when outside. Also, if outside a lot, cover the rest of your skin with long pants and shirts. It will be hot, so wear a fabric that "breathes," such as cotton.

Here are other tips that will stave off the look of aging and keep your skin in tip top shape:

- **Hydrate!!!** Drink at least eight glasses of water daily. Avoid caffeinated beverages as your sole source of hydration as well as mineral water and club soda. It's OK to drink your coffee in the morning but refrain from having it throughout the day. I can assure you that if you get in the habit of drinking water, you'll learn to like it. Eventually, you'll want it to quench your thirst. Try some herbal teas as an alternative.
- **Take supplements such as C and E, as well as essential fatty acids that are rich in the Omega 3s.**
- **Get plenty of rest!** Sleep is nature's repair shop. If you don't have enough sleep, it will show all over your face and over time promotes aging. As well, research has shown that a lack of sleep promotes unnecessary hunger and eating, and in time, will add unwanted weight!
- **Reduce stress.** This is not easy, I know that. The heart palpitations, the sweaty palms, the anxiety and frustration are part of our response to stress, and this takes its toll on our hearts, arteries and skin. I suggest incorporating yoga as a vehicle to exercise, relax and reduce stress. Yoga helps develop your breathing, which ultimately aids in stress reduction. There are many, many kinds of yoga out there; find the one that's best for you. Besides, yoga helps you to tone, stretch and strengthen your body.

- **Exercise.** Did you know that when you get the blood flowing, the increased circulation helps to aid the skin and ward off wrinkles?
- **Don't smoke.** Inhaling smoke constricts the blood vessels, and this promotes aging as well as other problems that we are well aware of.
- **Minimize alcohol.** Moderation is the key.
- **Wear sunglasses.** This protects your eyes and the skin around them.
- **Moisturize hands with a lotion and sun block throughout the day.**
- **Get into the habit of a daily skin care regime.** No matter what your age is, create a routine of cleansing, moisturizing and protecting your skin morning and night. Avoid soap and cleanse with a soap-free cleanser. (Even soaps that claim to be moisturizing bars are predominately soap.) After cleansing, use a toner such as witch hazel or alcohol-free products. (If you have sensitive skin, you'll want to avoid alcohol at all costs; this will really irritate your skin.) After that, moisturize and protect with a sun block.

When choosing products to care for the skin, price is NOT an indicator of better quality. There are some creams that are more than $100 a jar and do no better than a $5 jar. Check the ingredients, especially if you have sensitive skin. Ask your dermatologist or aesthetician about the products they recommend.

Skin Types

Everyone's skin is different; however, they fall into five categories with specific concerns and needs. They are normal, oily, dry, sensitive and combination.

- **Normal**: Normal skin is just that; it is neither overly dry nor oily. The sebaceous glands secrete enough oil, and the oil is distributed evenly throughout the skin. A good basic cleanser, a toner and a moisturizer with sun block are all you really need. Realize, however, that as you age, your skin will become drier;

so be prepared to move towards a heavier moisturizer down the road.

- **Oily**: Oily skin is produced when the sebaceous glands are working overtime, and they secrete too much oil that builds up on the face. Many times, those with oily skin are prone to acne or pimples because of this. It's still important to cleanse, moisturize and protect; however, the products should be oil-free. Often, people will use alcohol and drying products on their skin and wonder why they still keep breaking out. It's because the skin is dried out and just a little bit of oil results in pimples. But if you have oily skin, you are blessed, too. As your skin ages, the glands will not produce as much oil and your skin will become normal. As well, because of the oil, wrinkles will not appear as early in life as with other skin types.

- **Dry**: Dry skin is the result of the sebaceous glands not producing enough oil or as a result of living in a dry climate, hormonal imbalances or acne treatments. You know you have dry skin because it is itchy, taunt and hurts and NEEDS to be moisturized to soothe it. It's critical to cleanse, moisturize and protect your skin with products that are appropriate for this type. Realize, as well, that when you age, if you had dry skin as a youth that it will become dryer and more moisture will be necessary. Also dry skin has a tendency to wrinkle sooner than the other skin types.

- **Sensitive:** Sensitive skin is just that – it tends to get irritated easily. Perfumes, alcohol and makeup remover solutions have a tendency to irritate this type of skin. If this is your skin type, you'll want to avoid them. Look for cleansers that are soap-free, as well as moisturizers and protectors that are hypoallergenic. Finally, remove makeup with olive or mineral oil.

- **Combination:** Combination skin is the result of an unbalanced production of oil and an uneven distribution of oil throughout the skin. In the face, the oilier sections are most often found in the forehead, nose and chin, called the T-Zone. Combination skin can be the result of hormones or genetics; however, in caring for it, it's still important to cleanse, moisturize and protect the skin daily. You may consider adding a toner, such as witch hazel, and applying it after cleansing to balance the PH of the skin before moisturizing.

If you get into the routine of cleansing, moisturizing and protecting your skin, you will minimize the impact of the environmental factors that really age your skin – but you can still do more. As you get into your 30s, you'll want to incorporate another step at least once a week. At this stage, the skin is not regenerating at quite the speed it used to in your younger years so it will be important to help the skin exfoliate excess cells and particles. Exfoliation can be as simple as using cleansing cloths to exfoliating creams. Find one that works for your skin type, and avoid those that are too abrasive over your face. They can be too harsh and damage the epidermis. This is especially true as you age, since the skin, even in your 40s, gets thinner and starts drying out.

Skin Care for Men

This is a growing market but an essential one. Men need to take care of their skin since they're more likely to be outdoors in the sun and they shave regularly. Men's facial skin, in particular, is different from women. Obviously, men have more hair but also they have more sebaceous glands and thus prone to breakouts. As well, men's skin has a tendency to have more yeast that can also make them candidates for dry, red and flaky skin. Men need to get in the habit of moisturizing their face since shaving reduces moisture.

One of the problems that many men who shave have is razor bumps or pseudofolliculitis. This is when facial hairs curl back on themselves and back into the skin, and it's a condition that is particularly common with African American men. To minimize this condition, follow these steps:

- Take a hot shower to soften the hair and open the pores.
- Use a thick shave gel.
- Minimize stretching the skin when shaving.
- Shave in one direction and limit the number of strokes.

If you get razor bumps, consider using a clean needle to get the hair out. If this is a recurring problem, consider using depilatories (hair removal preparations); however, be warned, they are extremely irritating. Another option would be applying hydrocortisone cream to the affected area and if that doesn't work, it might be time to get some antibiotics or a prescription from your doctor. Another option is laser treatments that are designed to reduce the number of bumps that form; however, be prepared for several treatments rather than a one-shot fix.

Common Skin Problems and Their Remedies

A perfect complexion is nonexistent. Most people have problems with their skin of some nature; however, as we age, these problems become more prevalent. Enlarged pores, tiny fatty deposits or lipomas, clogged oil glands or sebaceous hyperplasia are just some of the things that start showing up. Consider a monthly facial from a licensed aesthetician. Some other common problems that affect the skin include adult acne, rosacea , hyperpigmentation and hypopigmentation. Let's take a look at this latter group:

- **Adult Acne**: And we thought acne was confined to our teenage years! Many adults are surprised to discover it also showing up in adulthood. Essentially, acne is when the sebaceous glands produce too much oil and the pores get clogged, resulting in swelling and inflammation. This condition is not caused by bacteria. Some of the causes of adult acne include living in a humid climate, hormonal changes and the use of steroids. To deal with this condition, consider products with benzoyl peroxide or salicylic acid, and look for noncomedogenic products or those that won't clog your pores. Minimize the use of hats and headbands and keep hair off the face. When cleansing the skin, avoid scrubbing and repeated washings since drying the skin out will only make it more prone to breaking out. Follow cleansing with a moisturizer that has sun block to protect the skin. Consider exfoliating the skin at least once a week. If the problem continues, consider taking an oral antibiotic, such as tetracycline, utilizing a cream that has retinol in it, and/or trying some natural options such as tea tree oil or vitamin B5. Another option is phototherapy that uses lasers to help clear the skin and reduce scarring.
- **Rosacea** is a chronic condition resulting in inflammation of

the cheeks, nose, chin, forehead and eyelids. It usually occurs between the ages of 30 to 50, to those who are fair-skinned, and mostly to women. Essentially, the blood vessels under the skin become irritated and inflamed and the triggers vary. At this point, not much is known about the condition but a common result of rosacea is a bulbous nose. To minimize the outward affects of this chronic skin condition, avoid sun exposure and limit spicy food, alcohol and hot beverages. To minimize redness, consider laser surgery/treatments.

- **Hyperpigmentation**: Also known as melasma, freckles, age spots, and sun/liver spots, this is a darkening of the skin, and it can be the result of pregnancy, acne, oral contraceptive use, and sun damage. If you had freckles as a youth, unfortunately, as you age the spots will darken. Some of the remedies to lessen the look of hyperpigmentation include OTC topical lightening products, chemical peels and laser treatments. However, to use any of these treatments, it is necessary to avoid the sun at all costs. Wear a sun block and a hat if possible when outdoors, and avoid being outside during the mid part of the day when the sun is the strongest.
- **Hypopigmentation** is the opposite of hyperpigmentation, and it is caused by injury to the skin such as a burn, trauma or from an autoimmune disease. A genetic disorder also results in a type of hypopigmentation known as albinism. However, if the skin has been affected by trauma or an autoimmune disease, the skin forms white blotches where the injury occurred or throughout. To remedy this, use sunless tanning products.

And the Rest of the Body?

It's not only important to take care of the face but also the skin that covers the rest of our body. If your skin has a tendency to be dry, avoid hot prolonged showers which will only accentuate the problem. Make sure to moisturize your whole body daily to avoid itchy and scratchy skin.

Your skin's needs will vary throughout the year and this depends also on where you live. For example, during the winter, the skin needs more moisture; you may want to introduce lotions and cream or oil-based shower gels during this period. Choose a body wash that does not contain soap since they can be drying. During the summer, a light moisturizer with sun care protection will be needed. If you live in a dry climate, you will need to step up your moisturizer to accommodate the lack of dampness in the air. As well, if you live in a humid climate, a lighter moisturizer may be all that is needed.

When bathing, use a wash cloth or shower puff to exfoliate the skin as well as body washes and gels. Soaps can be drying and leave a film on the body that can be irritating to the skin. Cleanse the body daily to avoid the build-up of dirt and bacteria. Use either a deodorant or antiperspirant to minimize odor and perspiration. Realize that deodorants simply minimize odor while antiperspirants minimize underarm perspiration.

However, if deodorants and antiperspirants don't work, you may have a condition called *hyperhidrosis* or excessive sweating. This occurs under the arms but also can be experienced in the hands and face. Excessive sweating is not related to nerves or temperatures but may be a result of a thyroid problem, diabetes or infection, so seek the advice of your health care professional for treatment. If you experience excessive sweating under the arms, consider a clinical strength antiperspirant and apply it at night and then in the morning. If this doesn't work, your doctor may recommend botox treatments that last for six months. Finally, if botox doesn't work, the doctor can perform surgery to stop the excessive sweating. This will not eliminate common perspiration so it will still be important to wear deodorants or antiperspirants.

Also, when it comes to your body, make sure to shampoo and condition your hair at least weekly. If you have oily hair or its summer, you may need to wash it more often. Consider shampoos that are sulfate-free if you have coarse or frizzy hair and volumizing shampoos if it's thin and fine. It doesn't matter if you're male or female; once you hit your 40s, you will lose some of your hair and it will start to thin. For some, this can result in baldness. No matter what, don't try to cover the problem with a part on the side of your head otherwise – known as the "comb over." Try to minimize stress on the scalp and hair with a good haircut and head massages.

In addition to thinning hair, you may find that hair starts growing where you don't want it to be. Because of the changes in our hormones, women can become more prone to facial hair. Consider laser therapy to remedy this and avoid shaving since this will only promote it. For men as they mature, hair starts to grow more coarse and thick out of the nose, ears and along the eyebrows. Consider having these areas trimmed each time you have your hair cut or purchase an electric shaver designed for nose and ear hair.

As well, when it comes to skin care, get a manicure weekly and a pedicure monthly. Your hands are part of your overall appearance at work. For example, if you are in the tech industry or in a supervisory position, dirty nails work against you. If you can't afford to pay for a manicure or pedicure, learn to do these yourself. You'll want to make sure that the nails and cuticles are clean, shaped and smooth. For men, buff your nails for sheen and luster, and for women, keep the nail polish simple without a lot of designs. I also advocate a pedicure because it helps to keep your feet soft and free from calluses; pedicures also deal with any potential problems, such as ingrown toenails.

Moreover, as we mature, our feet lose their padding and become easily callused and cracked – especially around the heels. Consider smoothing petroleum jelly on the feet nightly and wearing socks to keep them soft and free from cracks. The severity of this condition increases during the winter; so think about applying petroleum jelly, wrapping your feet in plastic wrap, and pulling on a pair of socks at night. This should resolve the problem in about three days.

Conclusion

Your skin is your greatest defender against bacteria and other diseases that can enter the body through its outer surface. Take care of your skin and it will take care of you!

13

Good Quality, The Right Fit

Buying quality clothing that fits without empting the bank account is a challenge with so many different kinds of stores and millions of brand names. Becoming a smart shopper takes time because it requires the development of skills; skills that will enable you to make the right purchases that build your wardrobe instead of just emptying your wallet.

As well, it is difficult to know if something fits or doesn't. Am I a small, medium, large or extra large? With most clothing items designed to fit a mannequin rather than a human being it's hard to know if the pants, shirt, dress or skirt we're trying on fits us correctly. We often find ourselves asking . . . is this supposed to be tight or loose like this?

Buying Quality

In the retail world, it's easy to get confused about what is a good deal with everything being on sale or promoted. Things have changed in the past 20 years, and retailers are under more pressure than ever to get results NOW. Years ago, a sale truly meant a sale; however, today it is not a sale unless it's a mark down on clearance merchandise. Most merchandise that is 10, 20 or even 40 percent off the regular price is a decrease in the markup rather than a mark down. Apparel and shoes have an average markup of 50, 70, 100 percent or more; so when there is a promotion where the sale of regular merchandise is 20 percent off, the retailer will still be making a profit. When certain styles are in fashion, the markup can be even higher – such as jeans with a markup of 700 percent or more! The markup for jeans has surpassed jewelry, which was notorious for having a markup of 300 percent or more.

When shopping, it's important to be vigilant about promotional offers – read the fine print. For example, oftentimes the retailer will match the competitor's price for the same item – but only if they sold the same model! Often it is the same; however, it will have a different model number based on the specific retailer. Sometimes there are deals where you can buy one and get the second for 50 percent off. That's a good deal if it's something that you want; however, it only encourages spending more. Use coupons and membership discounts to reduce your bill and get what you want, rather than getting something just because it's on sale.

When buying online, choose reputable retailers that have a history online or in brick and mortar form. There are lots of websites out there, and some may be counterfeit and you won't know until you've paid and never receive the merchandise. As well, be cautious if you see a great price on designer fragrances and bags, or anything in demand as they may be fakes. The counterfeit industry is huge with much of it being imported from China, which is the same country we get a lot of our clothing from. Some of your large retailers have been caught with counterfeit merchandise unknowingly, so this problem has plagued retailers as well. As they say, if it's too good to be true, it probably is.

Additional Tips for Quality

Here are some more tips that you can use during your next shopping venture. They will help clear the jungle in the fashion retail world!

- **Set some goals and objectives and be specific.** When you organize your closet (Chapter 3) you'll know what you have and be able to identify the key pieces needed to pull your wardrobe together or update it. Further, write these items down, along with the price you're willing to pay. This will reduce any impulse buying.
- **Haste makes waste.** Don't be in a hurry and give yourself enough time to evaluate the item before buying.
- **Be aware of current fashion trends.** Familiarize yourself with specific style names, such as double-breasted, fitted shirts,

shirt waist dresses and bomber jackets (many of these terms are explained in the Glossary). This way, you'll be able to communicate to the salesperson in a clear manner that they'll understand. If you're online, knowing the terms will help in your search as well.

- **If visiting a brick and mortar store, dress for the shopping venture.** For example, if a woman plans to purchase evening attire, she'll want to remember to wear or bring along the appropriate undergarments and shoes. Dress comfortably and wear shoes that will be comfortable over a long period of time.

- **Trying to match or coordinate with an item of clothing from your wardrobe?** If so, cut a swatch from the seam allowance of the garment and bring it with you. This will help you and the salesperson locate the right-colored item.

- **Shop alone.** This may seem like a difficult task, but it's the wise thing to do. When you shop with a friend, you may end up purchasing something you had no intention of buying. If you see something, put it on hold and come back to examine it.

- **Sometimes living partners have an arrangement where nothing is purchased without the other's say-so.** If this is the case, you might pick out the item you wish to purchase, put it on hold (or in your shopping bag, if online,) and then bring your partner back to OK the purchase.

- **Men should consider doing their own shopping, rather than having it done by their girlfriend, spouse and certainly not the administrative assistant!** Know your measurements and your likes and dislikes when venturing out to stores or online so that you can make satisfactory purchases.

- **If you can, try on all items before purchasing them since sizing is not uniform in the apparel industry.** A lot of variation can be found within a single brand or size; however, realize that higher-priced clothing can be generous in size.

- **Examine the item carefully for quality in the store or when it first arrives to your house.** Check for fabric flaws, stains, workmanship, unraveling hems, seam allowances and missing buttons.

- **If at a store when trying things on, go outside the dressing**

room for a more accurate look in the mirror. The lighting in the dressing room often promotes an inaccurate evaluation of the clothing item with your skin color.

- **Buy shoes in the afternoon because feet swell as the day progresses.** If buying online, keep to the brands that you know fit right the first time.

- **Don't neglect to buy accessories to complete your outfit.** This could include hosiery, belts, pocket squares or jewelry.

- **Know the retailer's return policies.** If it's clearance merchandise, you may not be able to return it. Further, you may only be able to get a store or merchandise credit, rather than your money back, depending how you paid for it and if you had your receipt.

- **Check the fiber content and garment care before buying to make sure it fits with your style of cleaning clothes.** If you're not big on dry cleaning, avoid care labels that say "professionally dry clean only."

- **See if there's a warranty or guarantee with some of your more expensive purchases, such as bags and if the warranty/ guarantee is worth the price.** For example, with some brands of handbags, you can return the item (if you've registered it) at any time and they will repair or replace it.

- **When evaluating plaid or striped garments, check to make sure that the stripes and plaids line up at the front, side and back seams.** This could also involve the sleeve, leg and shoulder seams as well, depending on what you're buying.

- **If evaluating suit or any two-piece outfit, check to make sure that the top and bottom of the outfit are the same color.** When fabric is dyed, certain yardage of it is placed in a large dye bath, and then put on bolts. This process is repeated until the specified amount of dyed fabric is completed. However, sometimes the fabric does not absorb the dye in the same manner as before, resulting in fabrics that differ slightly in color. This can happen to any manufacturer; so even when the label spells quality to you, make sure to compare both items for color quality.

- **Check seam allowances to make sure the seams are finished**

to some degree. If the garment is not lined, body movements put wear and tear on the interior of the garment and unfinished seams will unravel. This will begin as soon as the garment is laundered; so examine the seam allowance for some kind of finish such as zigzag stitching, pinked, turned under, or stitching. This should be apparent on knit as well as woven garments.

- **Check seams for puckering.** When garments are sewn in factories, many fabrics are run though the same sewing machine without any adjustment to tension; this can result in puckering. You can't iron it out and it will ultimately affect the hang of the garment.

- **Check the buttons for secure attachment and appearance.** To curtail costs, many manufacturers cut down on thread. Check each button to make sure thread is running through every attaching hole. Tug on them slightly to see whether they are loose. If you don't mind replacing loose buttons, purchase the garment anyway; however, don't expect it to last a long time. Check to see whether extra buttons come with the garment. If not, check with the salesperson; the department may have a drawer full. While you're at it, check every button to make sure it is not cracked, chipped or broken. Further, make sure zippers ride easily when opening or closing them.

- **Check the pockets for quality.** Inseam pockets are often a combination of the fashion fabric and the lining, usually in cotton, acetate or nylon. If you can see the lining when you try on the garment perhaps at the hem or at the side pocket, don't buy it. Apparently the fashion fabric did not go far enough into the pocket or the lining was not attached correctly at the waist or the hem is out. Make sure, too, that the lining compliments the fashion fabric and does not show through. For example, thick lining fabrics add extra bulk, which will be apparent. Navy lining with light colored pants is hard to ignore. Linings in pants, jackets and skirts are attached at the waist and hemmed separately.

- **When purchasing a gathered garment, look for a consistent**

flow of gathers. Or if the garment is pleated, be sure the pleats are evenly spaced and alike in pleat width and depth.

- **Check buttonholes for quality.** They should be even, with closely spaced stitches and no loose threads.
- **With shoes, make sure that the upper leather is attached securely to the sole.** Also, note whether the seams are straight.
- **Any decorative details, such as top stitching, should be straight and without flaws.**
- **The interfacing should lie smoothly.** Interfacings are used to provide extra body and support to collars, cuffs, waistbands, shirt front plackets, and jacket lapels. To keep costs down, many manufacturers use a synthetic called "pelon," that is heat set on the fabric. Sometimes the heat is not applied properly and the interfacing pulls away from the fabric. This can create bubbles in the fabric, so be on the lookout. Check also to make sure that the interfacing is of an appropriate stiffness for the fashion fabric. For example, putting a very stiff interfacing with a soft rayon fabric women's blouse will ruin the drape of the fabric.
- **Check the hang of the garment to be sure that it was sewn on the lengthwise grain of the fabric.** For example, when side seams on trousers, jeans or even jackets shift toward the front, the fabric was not cut on the grain.
- **When shopping for good bargains, consider second hand, thrift or consignment shops and off-priced stores in addition to mass merchants, department and specialty stores.** Manufacturer and designer outlets are also viable options; however, realize that in those stores they are most likely selling surplus merchandise, seconds and irregulars.
- **If you cannot find clothing that fits or you have special needs, there are companies that will make it for you at a price that's affordable.** For custom clothing, check out Noble House (http://noblehouse.us/), Ravis Tailor (www.ravistailor. com), Dara Lamb (for women at www.daralamb.com), J. Hillburn (www.jhillburn.com) and Individually Suited (www. individuallysuited.com). Regarding special needs apparel for those with disabilities, consider Silverts (www.silverts.com),

Professional Fit (www.professionalfit.com), and Able 2 Wear (www.able2wear.co.uk) as online companies that specialize in this area.

Getting the Right Fit

Part of buying quality that's worth the price is the fit of the garment on you. Nothing looks cheaper than wearing something that's too big or too small. If you've gained weight, acknowledge it and seek to enhance your body with clothing that fits. Otherwise you'll just be drawing attention to the problem. There's no standardized sizing in the apparel industry, with one brand you may wear a 12 and in another a 16 and in yet another a 10. How can you figure out what size you wear? Here's the answer … rather than focusing on the SIZE you wear, try to fit your body. However, most people don't know what fits them.

Clothing today has a multitude of fit categories from *close fit, fitted, semi fitted* to *loose* and *very loose fitting*. What do these mean when you're trying to find a fitted shirt? Close fit implies that the garment follows closely the curves of the body, while fitted is slightly more relaxed. Semi fitted has even more ease than the other two, while loose fitting indicates a garment that is generously sized with ease of movement and fabric drape. Finally, very loose fitting is a full garment with lots of ease, and it provides the ultimate in comfort.

As well, when purchasing jeans, there are various categories to select from that include *traditional, slim, relaxed* and *loose*. Traditional cut is essentially true to size while slim is cut narrower, especially in the legs and hips. Relaxed jeans have an extra half an inch in the seat and thighs. Meanwhile, loose fit has one to four inches of ease in the butt and thighs.

When shopping and trying clothes on, be honest with yourself regarding the fit since we are NOT a dress form. Realize that it can be a challenge to find the right fit. However, it will make a world of difference in how you look in your clothes for work and how you feel about yourself.

Here are some tips to help ensure that you have the right fit *for you*:

- **When buying a belt, if you have a 34 inch waist, buy a 36**

inch belt. The belt should fasten on the center hole with the tail ending right past the first loop on the pants.

- **Jackets, blazers and sport coats for men should cover the back side and close comfortably in front.** Sleeves should land about one-half inch below the wrist bone. The jacket should hang straight at the side and back seams and not pull. Shoulder seams need to land about one half inch from the shoulder bone.

- **For women, jackets and blazers (depending on the style) should land straight without gapping or puckering on the sides or back.** You should be able to button it with the sleeves landing one-fourth to one-half inch below the wrist bone. Like men, if it's a set in the sleeve, the shoulder seam should land about one-half inch beyond the shoulder bone.

- **Men's shirts should be able to close comfortably, allowing one finger's worth of ease in the neck and no gapping or wrinkling there.** If wearing your shirt out, it should hang at the end of the zipper of your pants and at the pant pockets in the back. If wearing a shirt with a jacket, it should peek out about one-half inch beyond the jacket sleeve, essentially reaching the beginning of the thumb. Make sure that the shirt hangs straight at the front and sides and that there is ample ease in the sleeves for the arms.

- **Women's shirts, blouses and tops also need to hang straight at the front and sides without gapping and wrinkling at the neck.** If it has a set-in sleeve, the seam should land at the shoulder bone. The sleeve length, if long, should be about one-half inch beyond the wrist bone. Tightness under the arms as well as through the back and front means that the top is too small.

- **Pants should have ample ease of one to four inches through the seat, hips, waist and thighs.** If the pants are pleated, they should lay flat. If there is a crease down the front leg of the pant, it should fall straight. Regarding length, try your pants on without shoes, they should just touch the floor.

- **For men, some indications of pants that don't fit are too much fabric in the seat, the stomach extending over the**

waist, pants righting on the hips or tightness in the thigh.
Tightness in the rear also indicates that pants don't fit. If there is too much fabric in the seat of the pants, have the excess removed. Pants should ride over the hip and thigh area with enough ease to allow freedom of movement. The side seam of the pant should hang straight down the side. Finally, inseam pockets should not spread apart to show the lining.

- **For women, the rules for pants are about the same but with a few more considerations.** Pants should have ample ease in the waist, hips and thighs. Pants are too tight if when you close the pants, excess skin bulges out creating a "muffin top." There should be ample ease in the crotch so that the seam does not pull or in the derriere to outline your "cheeks." If the fabric stretches around the thighs, the pants are too small. The side seams should hang straight down the side, and the pants should touch the floor when standing in them in your bare feet.

- **Skirts should have one to two inches of ease in the waist, hips and thighs and not pull across the belly.** The hem of the skirt should be parallel to the floor. Side seams should hang straight and the skirt should not ride up in the front or back.

- **Shoes should fit comfortably the first time.** Remember when you were small and the salesperson would measure your feet and press his index finger to make sure you had enough room at the front of the shoe? Those steps are just as important today. Don't be fooled by the line that the shoes will become more comfortable as you wear them or that once you break them in they will be enjoyable to wear all day long – WRONG. Shoes should fit comfortably the first time, every time. If your shoes don't fit, your attitude won't be very fitting either!

- **To check the shoe size, stand with your feet spread apart, equal weight placed on each foot.** There should be an index-finger's space between your longest toe and the end of the shoe. Make sure the widest part of your foot lines up with the widest part of the shoe. Try on shoes with the proper hosiery. If you're trying on running shoes, wear athletic socks. If you're a woman trying on pumps, bring along knee-highs. Most shoes stores have hosiery if you forget. Even if you don't plan to wear hosiery, they will aid in determining the fit of the shoe to your foot.

- **Proper length is essential.** If the pants are to be tailored, wear the shoes that you intend to wear with them. The pants should fall straight, with a slight break at the top of the shoe. At the back of the pant, the hem should land at the point or slightly above where the sole and upper leather meet. This results in pants that are slightly longer in the back (about three-quarters of an inch) than in front. Pant hems should not touch the ground since it will destroy the fabric and your investment. Cuffed pants should hang horizontally and be about one and one-half inch in width.
- **Skirt length extremes should be avoided.** However, when determining the length, the most attractive length and one used by many designers is right around the knee.

Bottom line: Clothing that doesn't fit draws attention to the problem. If the item fits in one place but not another, it doesn't fit. If it's uncomfortable to sit or move freely, it's too tight. Realize also, however, that if your clothing is too big, this also draws the eye to the problem. Signs that clothing is too large include pants falling off the waist, jackets and t-shirts looking oversized, or pants dragging on the ground. Seek clothing that fits your body, and you'll look good and be able to move freely and comfortably at work.

Conclusion

Knowing how to buy quality and knowing what fits makes every dollar count in a way that benefits you and your finite clothing budget. Make your dollar go further by making purchases that take your professional image where *you* want it to go!

14

A Word to Employers

Part of marketing your business is developing and delivering a consistent image of what your company stands for. A lot of time goes into planning the location, company/store atmosphere, and product/service mix. Part of delivering your image is also through your employees. Whether it is on the phone, through the Internet, or in person, it's essential that your product offering be delivered through these contact points in a consistent manner that enhances your brand image. Particularly in service-oriented businesses, consistency is hard to maintain since people are the foundation for delivering it. It's even more important in these types of businesses to establish policies to enhance consistency and maintain the image of your business.

As mentioned earlier, Attribution Theory purports that people make inferences about others on very little information. With people, it is their appearance that is the predominant factor. So when it comes to sending a consistent image, no matter what your type or size of business, a written dress policy that is followed will help your employees know where they stand.

Dress in the past was much more formal than it is today. In the 80s and 90s, a lot of companies introduced "Casual Friday," and a decade later, many retracted it because casual became sloppy. Moreover, the technology revolution, along with an increase in cultural and religious diversity, has resulted in many working adults without knowledge of what is appropriate for work. As a business owner, understand that employees will most likely take their cue from what you wear. So if appearance is important in enhancing the corporate image, be a role model and implement a dress policy.

Having a company dress policy offers many benefits to employers and their workers. First, it enhances safety in the workplace by avoiding clothing that could be hazardous when working with company equipment. In addition, it lessens the possibility of an employee wearing clothing that has negative inferences. A dress policy also promotes an atmosphere of team work at your workplace, and it helps develops personal pride and professionalism in your employees. As well, the policy helps employees operate freely without sexual harassment or favoritism based on provocative dress. Lastly, such a policy, when in place, ensures what is expected in the workplace and protects the business by limiting workman's compensation expenditures. Many, many companies have written dress policies – schools and universities, construction and manufacturing entities, small stores and large corporations. A written dress policy helps you to be a better employer, running a business that has integrity and is professionally managed.

Considerations for a Dress Policy

Written dress policies vary, depending on your corporate/business environment, from very formal to very informal. Such a policy should be inclusive to not only cover clothing but accessories as well, especially when employee safety is a concern.

In developing a dress policy, here are some tips to ensure that yours will reflect the needs of your business:

- **Include employees at all levels when putting together a team to formulate the company dress policy.** This will aid in developing one that is comprehensive in scope.
- **Understand all aspects of your business operations.** Is safety an issue? For example, if on a construction site, are steel-tip shoes necessary to ensure that feet are protected? As well, are earring or hair length requirements necessary to avoid hair and jewelry from getting caught in the equipment?
- **Understand what has been a problem regarding dress at your business, and address it in the dress policy.** If an employee's hygiene has been a problem, spell out what is acceptable for your business.
- **Know clearly what your business stands for and your**

competitive advantage. Be able to identify the different contact/touch points that employees have with customers, suppliers and the public.

- **Does the company have different areas of operations – such as manufacturing, office and outside sales?** Address all areas regarding appropriate and inappropriate attire.
- **Be clear on what's acceptable and unacceptable regarding clothing, accessories and hygiene.** Give examples of clothing items that are appropriate and those that are not.
- **Understand federal rulings on what is allowed by law.** In the US, the courts have ruled that employers may enforce appearance rules even if they prohibit the expression of cultural or ethnic values if the rules are reasonable, job-related, and applied consistently. For example, an employer can require men to have short hair, women to wear make-up, or employees to cover tattoos and piercings in the workplace just as long as the policy is applied to everyone equally. Become familiar with Title VII of the Civil Rights Act and the issue of trait discrimination when developing a policy to be assured of a policy that is free of legal ramifications.
- **Be sensitive to implied or explicit policies that show favoritism to one group over another by race, gender, ethnicity or disability.** For example, banning ponytails for men but allowing it for women is discriminatory. As well, banning facial hair is discriminatory against African American males, due to problems related to shaving that are not commonly found with other races or ethnic groups. Moreover, it is prohibited to require an employee to wear a sexually provocative uniform or to mandate that women dress in a feminine way (such as wearing skirts).
- **Delineate the steps to be taken when the dress policy is not followed.** Know what can and cannot be done and what you are willing to do to enforce it. Usually, the first infraction is a written warning given to the employee on the day that the item is worn. Each additional infraction should be of greater consequence to the employee. However it is enforced, each infraction should be documented in the employee file.

- Consider implementing the new dress policy on a three-month trial basis.
- Once the dress policy is finalized, communicate it to all employees and make sure that it is part of the company handbook. New employees should become knowledgeable of the policy once they're hired. Consider having employees sign off on the dress policy, indicating that they will follow it.

No matter what your business climate, whether formal or informal, a dress policy should be part of the company mode of operations.

What about Uniforms?

As an option, uniforms are beneficial since they identify employees to the public and enhance hygiene and safety needs for the employer. If uniforms are required for all employees, the dress policy needs to address the condition of the uniform and the company's responsibility should it become torn or ill-fitting. If the uniform has the company's logo on them, then the employer is responsible for paying for them and providing them to employees. In some cases a deposit may be required from employees that would be returned when the uniforms are returned. However, if the dress policy requires that each employee wear a red top and khaki bottom that can be worn elsewhere, as in the case of Target, the business is not obligated to subsidize the employee for this.

With uniforms, the dress policy would likely address hygiene, jewelry, tattoos, body piercings, hosiery and shoes (if not provided). Further, if implementing uniforms for your business, will the conduct of the employee outside the business in the uniform be an issue? For example, would the employee be able to wear the uniform to and from work, and would they be able to drink alcoholic beverages in public with the uniform on?

Formal vs. Casual Dress Policies

A formal dress policy has many positive benefits. It communicates a business focus, and employees are perceived as intelligent by customers. However, the disadvantages are that employees can be perceived as too superior to customers, and such a formal policy may be inappropriate in some business settings.

As well, a casual policy can be perceived as a perk by employees, but your business image may suffer. Moreover, research found that when a casual policy was the norm, there was greater tardiness and absenteeism among employees. As well there was an increase in foul language used in the workplace.

When deciding what kind of dress policy to implement, consider first the image you want to communicate about your company to your customers. As well, consider the nature of the contact points that employees will have with customers. And finally, think about the work environment you want to create for your employees and customers to help get business done. Understanding these issues as it relates to your company will help you decide whether a formal or a casual dress code is right for your business.

Steps for Creating Your Policy

In writing your dress policy, follow these simple steps:

1. **Identify your company needs and how the dress policy will achieve the desired results.**
2. **Communicate what your company dress policy is and what that policy means.**
3. **List acceptable attire for men and women in explicit detail.** Break it down by categories, such as pants/skirts, suits, shirts/blouses, shoes/hosiery/socks, accessories and grooming.
4. **List unacceptable attire and hygienic habits for men and women.** Use the same categories to eliminate confusion.
5. **List how the policy will be enforced.**
6. **Finally, provide a statement to the effect that management is available to employees to discuss, in private, individual concerns and that every effort will be made to accommodate special situations.**

When it comes to company dress policies, clothing items that have typically been banned from the workplace have included tank tops, halter tops and dresses, muscle shirts, clothing with words, torn clothing, sweatpants and/or sweat suits, and hats. When it comes to hygiene, some concerns are body odor and the use of perfumes and colognes. More and more people are sensitive to chemicals in the air and so use of perfumes and colognes needs to be addressed.

Conclusion

When companies have written dress policies in the past, one problem has been not being explicit enough. Being abstract gives employees too much latitude and brings about abuses of the policy, resulting in a negative business environment. Hence, it's important for employers to decide what their company stands for and the desired business climate they want to achieve with employees and customers.

Given this, consider using the categories defined in this book (suits required, jackets optional and jeans permitted) to give employees a true sense of what's appropriate clothing in the workplace. Such terms as formal, informal or even business casual are vague and provide for a multitude of interpretations among businesses and employees. More than ever, employers cannot rest on the assumption that employees will understand what is required when these terms are used.

In today's business world, your brand image is important to its success. It works to the company's advantage to embrace a productive environment through explicit policies that set the tone to create and maintain a professional atmosphere. With a clear dress policy, employees will know what is expected at their place of employment as well as any business matter off the premises. Dress policies are more important than ever in today's business world. Such policies protect the business and its employees, so take the time to develop one that is clear and works for your company. You'll be glad you did.

15

It's More Than Just the Clothes You Wear

Throughout this book, I've talked about a new definition of business dress and discussed various components in achieving a professional appearance for the workplace. However, it takes more than the clothes you wear when it comes to your ability to get things done and to project a professional image that will support your career success.

One aspect of appearance that is just as important as the clothes you wear is your body language. You could have the greatest outfit on; however, if you're avoiding eye contact or are slouching in your chair, you might do as well being naked because you can destroy any advantage that your clothing are providing. Be aware of your body language; it speaks louder than the words you use. Nonverbal communication accounts for over 50 percent of the meaning derived in overall communication, and it's even more important in first impression situations. Even when you haven't said a word, your body has been sending signals about you to others. If what you do say conflicts with these body messages, be warned: the recipient will perceive the nonverbal communication as true. In other words, your body speaks the truth.

Four Types of Body Motions

Body motions can be grouped into four types:

- **The first group is referred to as *emblems*.** These are widely accepted translations, such as a nod for yes and smiling as a sign for happiness.

- **The second group is made up of *illustrators*.** These accompany verbal messages to support a point. For example, when we say the number one, we might hold up one finger.

- **The third group consists of _regulators_.** These are movements that serve, either positively or negatively, to regulate conversation. For example, to regulate a conversation positively and move it along, the parties may maintain eye contact. When someone wants to end the conversation, he or she will look down, or turn his or her head or body away from the speaker, signaling that they have essentially checked out.

- **The fourth group is that of the _adaptors_.** Adaptive body motions help us to deal with feelings of uneasiness. They include nervous habits – such as twisting our hair, playing with our clothing, tugging our ears, or biting our nails – habits manifested in unfamiliar or uncomfortable situations. It's true that when people lie, they give one-third less eye contact and can be a bit agitated. The body has a difficult time telling a lie. In one way or another, through nervous ticks – such as tapping the foot, stroking the back of the neck, or shifting constantly in a chair – the individual will provide the clues nonverbally about the situation.

Increasing Awareness

The more that you're aware of your body language, the more you can send the right message about yourself and, in return, understand others better. Those individuals that we perceive as being very confident seem to stand or sit comfortably erect and give eye contact. Their gestures are warm and add to clarify their verbal message, rather than distract. Take time in front of a mirror to see how your body communicates so you will be aware of the nonverbal messages you're sending. Once you're aware, you will be able to communicate more effectively to others at work.

Here are some body motions and their meaning:

- **Rubbing your eyes** often means you're trying to avoid looking at someone, and it is seen as a behavior in someone who is being untruthful.

- **Pulling at the back or side of your collar** often communicates deceit and the feeling that someone is suspicious of you.
- **Gesturing with your thumb extended** sends a message of superiority and authority.
- **Clasping your hands behind your back** signals authority and superiority. This position is common among police officers and other authority figures.
- **Fiddling with loose change in your pocket**, whether you're listening or talking, indicates a concern for money. In a selling situation, the buyer is communicating a concern for how much the product or service costs.
- **Palms up** commonly demonstrate openness, acceptance of an idea, and participation.
- **A fist with the index finger pointed toward someone** generally commands submission from the person directed. This is one of the most condescending and irritating gestures available and thus it should be used sparingly.
- **Upturned fists** can draw the listener to you as well as reinforce a point aggressively.
- **Warm gestures** include leaning towards people when speaking or listening, facing them directly, smiling, touching and gesturing expressively.
- **Cold gestures** include placing your hands on your hips, slumping, avoiding eye contact, and not smiling.
- **Some gestures display nervousness**, such as cleaning your fingernails, drumming your fingers, fiddling with objects or jewelry, looking at your watch or phone, licking your lips, scratching your arms, clearing your throat excessively, and tugging your ears.
- **When giving a group presentation, maintain eye contact with your audience 75 to 85 percent of the time.** Then, in one-to-one conversations, strive for 50 percent of the time.
- **The eye-block gesture is used to communicate status or boredom.** This is when a coworker tilts her head back slightly and closes her eyes. Either she has blocked you out of the conversation or she feels superior to you.

- **Arms and legs uncrossed in a sitting position** communicate an open posture.
- **Someone who stands with a curved back and lowered gaze** communicates a feeling of inferiority. Meanwhile, someone who stands comfortably erect is self-assured.
- **Keeping the trunk and legs straight but turning the head away from the speaker, or supporting the head with the arm** usually suggests a person's interest is fading.
- **Rubbing hands together** quickly usually communicates excitement.
- **Chin stroking** sends a message that you're making a decision.
- **Scratching the back of your head** says that you don't understand what is being said.
- **Picking at imaginary lint** signals boredom or disagreement.
- **Straddling a chair or putting something between you and another person**, such as a fence, doorway, or car door, essentially means you're protecting yourself. This position is often taken by domineering types; however, if you want to overcome this situation, try sitting or standing behind the person who is dominating. They will be forced to change their position.
- **Readiness** can be communicated in a seated position by leaning forward with your hands on your legs and one foot in front of the other as if to take a step.
- **Supporting your weight on the armrests of your chair** commonly signals that you're about to leave.
- **Men display aggression in a number of ways.** Like women, men size each other up – usually when they're angled away from each other in a relaxed posture. They may place their hands on their hips or their thumbs in their belt. Men in this position are evaluating each other; however, overt conflict is unlikely.
- **A confrontation may be inevitable**, however, when two men face each other directly with their feet about shoulder-length apart, weight evenly distributed, and their hands on their hips or on their belt.
- **Holding both hands behind your head** communicates confidence, control and/or superiority. When someone

reprimands you in this manner, you might want to respond by mirroring the position.

- **Tilting your head down** signals disagreement, a negative attitude, or anger.
- **Avoid entering a person's intimate zone**, which ranges from zero to 18 inches around them. In business, interactions should take place among individuals' social zone, which is about four to seven feet around them.

Interpreting Body Language

Is body language universal? *Definitely not!* Nonverbal messages vary from culture to culture and depend on the situation. For example, in France, they generally stand very close to the individual they're talking with. In America, this would be perceived as offensive since they would seem to be in our intimate space. If conducting business in France, stepping back might be perceived as an insult to this person. Hence, we need to be knowledgeable of the varying spatial needs of different cultures.

Furthermore, it's important to note that when you're trying to understand someone's body language, you must read all the parts. Don't isolate someone's posture and assign meaning to it alone. Look at other gestures being used and give meaning to those as well. Body language is a total package, so try to practice positive messages with your body. For example, in a conversation, look at the other person, and nod in understanding. Or when sitting, lean slightly forward to communicate that you're listening.

The handshake tells so much about someone. Learn to give a firm handshakes, but not bone crushers. Keep shaking hands for about 3 to 4 seconds along with eye contact and a smile for a great beginning to any business introduction.

Learn to use gestures to accentuate what you're saying and are perceived as warm rather than cold and authoritative. And even if you don't feel confident or comfortable inside, you will communicate it on the outside.

It's important to consider the context of the body signals being sent. Perhaps you come in contact with someone whose arms are folded across his chest. If it's cold, he may just be trying to stay warm. However, in a warm room, this could be rightly projecting a defensive, uninviting message. So there may be unknown reasons behind the message you receive.

The Art of Etiquette

In addition to body language, how you conduct yourself with others is very important. Many aspiring people may have the skills but lack the ability to convey it. They are abusive, abrupt and irrespective of others' differences or concerns. For people like that, it really doesn't matter what you're wearing or what you know, you are hard to deal with. If you're rough around the edges, consider stepping back and mastering the art of etiquette. It will help you wherever you go and will probably propel your career faster than all the skills and knowledge you possess. Others will want to recommend or nominate you for the position or task because you're good at what you do and are easy to work with.

When we think of etiquette, visions of charm school float to the surface, but etiquette is not charm school; it's a set of guidelines for everyday living. Living ethically means respecting those around you, even if you feel that they don't deserve it! If we all practiced etiquette, I believe the world would be a kinder, gentler place to live in. By practicing etiquette, you can feel confident in new situations and concentrate on getting your work done or making the deal.

A lot has changed over the years in our society, including standards of appropriate behavior. One of the greatest changes influencing etiquette has been women working. Gentlemanly behavior is still in demand – but not at the office. A man pulling out a chair for a woman could be in big trouble at work. But then again, who opens the door these days, men or women? Often it's the junior officer or employee, male or female. Other times, its' whoever gets to the door first.

Another major change is the increase in cultural diversity in the workplace, which requires sensitivity to differences in practices and perception. However, remember that the US is a land of over 400 ethnicities, so embrace the difference and grow from it.

Take charge of your career, your business, and even your home by learning some of the keys to etiquette for the workplace. You'll find that work goes a lot smoother and you are moving ahead in your business and career. No matter how trivial, practicing etiquette in the workplace will make you much more effective as a coworker, manager or boss.

Here are some basic tips to help you operate smoothly at work and get the job done.

- **At a restaurant, treat the restaurant staff with respect.**
- **Understand that whoever did the inviting is the one that pays for the meal.**
- **Practice good table manners**, remembering that the napkin goes in the lap and you never talk with your mouth full. Get comfortable with formal table settings.
- **Give the guest the best seat at the table when sitting.**
- **At work, avoid gossip and don't be an attention seeker.**
- **Be positive and look at your glass as half full.**
- **Acknowledge the contributions of others at work.**
- **If leading a team, acknowledge and understand everyone's view before coming to a decision.** Seek consensus, rather than forcing a choice.
- **Introduce others and say something good about them that will spark the conversation.**
- **With mobile phones and smartphones, keep them on silent or vibrator when in a meeting.** Step out if the call is urgent. Don't check your email or other messages when in a meeting or talking to someone.
- **With smartphones, cut and paste the attachment** rather than sending it as a download.
- **When Instant Messaging (IM) at work, have a business screen name, and keep the conversation brief.** If the conversation drags on, you may need a face-to-face chat.
- **With IM, check to make sure that the other party is free to participate.**
- **Always be professional when using email, face time, or instant messaging.** Follow company policies and check your English before sending. Check for clarity, grammar, spelling and punctuation. Avoid slang as well as foul language.
- **Check with the person you're trying to reach regarding their preferred form of correspondence.**

- **Be cautious with the Reply All feature on email.**
- **Don't write an email or send an IM that contains anything you would not say in person.** Avoid using all capitals in your writing. Reply to emails in 24 hours.
- **Take pride in your work.**
- **Learn to listen to others, rather than focusing on what you're going to say NEXT.**
- **In a conversation, focus on facts rather than conjecture.**
- **Be responsive to coworkers.**
- **When conflicts arise, don't jump to conclusions, criticize or blame others.** As well, avoid taking the issue personally. Resolve issues quickly and once it's over, it's over.

As many have said before me, seek to understand rather than being understood. Show value to others around you and they will express it in return. Life is too short to be tied up with games and manipulation of others. Brown nosing at work doesn't get you anywhere and creates an uneasy work environment. Be a team player, giving attention to the well-being of the company rather than your own desires. Being honest and forthright, focusing on principles over personalities, creates the positive environment you desire.

Conclusion

Some say that clothes make the person. However, how they carry themselves in their clothes and how they conduct their interactions with others will secure the positive impression they're seeking.

May you have much success!

Glossary

Acetate: is a cellulose based textile that is dry spun and blended with other fibers to produce sheen in fabrics.

A-line skirt: is a skirt that is fitted at the hips and gradually widens towards the hem, giving the impression of the shape of a capital letter A. This also applies to dresses and coats that have similar shapes.

Ascot: there are two types of ascots 1) the **ascot scarf**, which is a square of silk loosely gathered around the neck and, 2) the **ascot tie,** common in menswear and has a pleated neckband that is worn either under or over the collar.

Bell-shaped silhouette: a silhouette made popular by Christian Dior in the 1950's that includes a full skirt and sleeves making the waist appear tiny.

Bermuda shorts: also known as walking shorts or dress shorts, are a particular type of short pants, widely worn as semi-casual attire by men and women. They got their name from their popularity in the country of Bermuda. The hem can be cuffed or un-cuffed, and land about one inch above the knee.

Blazer: resembles a suit coat but is cut more casually sometimes with patch pockets and metal buttons. Historically a blazer's cloth was usually durable (14oz.), because it was an outdoor jacket. Blazers are often worn as part of the uniform for airline pilots or members of a rowing team.

Boat-neck: also called a bateau neck, refers to a wide neckline that runs horizontally, front and back, almost to the shoulder points, and across the collarbone. It is traditionally used in nautically inspired sweaters and knitwear and was originally derived from sailors' blouses or sweaters, often with wide navy and white horizontal stripes.

Bomber jacket: is a garment originally created for pilots, which eventually became part of popular culture and apparel. It is long sleeved, lands at the waist and commonly has a zipped closure.

Boot cut leg: Pant legs that are tapered to the knee yet loosens around the ankle to accommodate a boot.

Brocade: a class of richly decorative shuttle-woven fabrics, often made in colored silks and with or without gold and silver threads. Brocade is typically woven on a draw loom. It is a supplementary weft technique, that is, the ornamental brocading is produced by a supplementary, non-structural, weft in addition to the standard weft that holds the warp threads together. The purpose of this is to give the appearance that the weave is actually embroidered on.

Button-down collar: is a collar that has points fastened down by buttons on the front of the shirt. They were originally introduced by retailer Brooks Brothers in 1896.

Chalk-striped: is a series of threads, not just one, used to create a stripe that resembles a stripe that is drawn with tailors chalk or rope. The width of the stripe varies it is always wider than the pin stripe.

Chanel jacket: is a style of jacket originally designed by Coco Chanel. The jacket has a box silhouette with three quarter length sleeves and is weighted on the bottom by a chain that is sewn is the hem. The jacket is collarless, lands at the high hip, with simple closures at the center.

Chiffon: is a fabric made from cotton, silk or synthetic fibers. Chiffon can be dyed to almost any shade if out of natural fibers but when made out of polyester it can be difficult to dye. On close inspection it resembles a fine net or mesh which gives chiffon translucent properties and is mostly used in evening wear.

City shorts: are women's pants that are generally cuffed and land at the knee or no more than three inches above it. They are worn at the office when jackets are optional is an acceptable mode of attire.

Clothes Valet: is an item of furniture where clothes can be hung and aired out. Typical features of valets include trouser hangers, jacket hangers, shoe bars, and a tray organizer for miscellaneous, day-to-day objects like wallets and keys.

Cotton Twill: is also referred to as Chino and is a twill fabric originally made of 100% cotton. Today it is also found in cotton-synthetic blends and common among such brands as Dockers.

Convertible collar: is a collar that is the part of a shirt, dress, coat, or blouse that fastens around the neck. A collar is differentiated from other necklines such as lapels, by being made from a separate piece of fabric, rather than a folded or cut part of the same piece of fabric used for the main body of the garment.

Cordovan: is a shade of burgundy and rose. The term was first coined in Spain

Cowl neck: is a high loose-fitting turnover collar used especially for sweaters and women's blouses.

Crew Neck: is a type of shirt or sweater that has a round neckline and no collar. Often worn with other layers the crew was originally developed in 1932 as an undergarment for football players.

Cropped Jacket: is worn primarily by women as a short version of a jacket that lands above the waist but below the breast. Cropped jacket styles vary from dressed up and form fitting to very casual depending on the fabrication and style detail.

Cropped pants: are pants that land below the knee about midcalf.

Cummerbund: is a broad waistband usually worn in place of a vest with men's formal dress clothes and adapted in various styles of women's clothes.

Day dress: is a garment consisting of a skirt with an attached bodice (or a matching bodice giving the effect of a one-piece garment) worn during the day such as two piece dress or shirtwaist dress.

Double Wrap Belt: is a belt that is designed to go around the waist twice.

Drop Waist Style: is a horizontal waistline that falls near the level of the upper hips. This balances the upper and lower body (for those that are short waisted) and adds the impression of height by lengthening the torso.

Gabardine: is a tough, tightly woven fabric used to make suits, overcoats, trousers uniforms, windbreakers, and other garments. The fiber used to make the fabric is traditionally worsted wool, but may also be cotton, polyester, or a blend. Gabardine is woven as a warp-faced steep or regular twill, with a prominent diagonal rib on the face and smooth surface on the back.

Gathered skirt: is a full skirt, also known as dirndl skirts. The term dirndl originated in Austria and Bavaria and described an everyday dress with an apron.

Gladiator sandals: are flat sandals that lace up the calf ending mid calf or right below the knee.

Glen Plaid: is a woolen fabric with a woven twill design of small and large checks also known as a Bankers Plaid because of the frequency of bankers wearing the pattern. The pattern has been introduced to cotton shirting and other non-woolen fabrics as well.

Herringbone pattern: describes a distinctive V-shaped weaving pattern usually found in twill fabric. The pattern is called herringbone because it resembles the skeleton of a herring fish. Herringbone-patterned fabric is usually wool and is one of the most popular cloths used for suits and outerwear. Tweed is often woven in a herringbone pattern.

Houndstooth: describes a check pattern that is made with alternating bands of four dark and four light threads in both warp and filling or weft woven in a simple 2:2 twill, two over - two under the warp, advancing one thread on each pass. The resulting pattern can be large or small depending on the needs of the designer.

Jeggings: are leggings that are made of denim and Lycra spandex to look like tight denim jeans.

Jewel neck: is a neckline that is round and sits at the base of the throat. It is also called the T-shirt neckline.

Linen: is a textile made from the fibers of the flax plant. Linen is labor-intensive to manufacture, but when it is made into garments, it is valued for its exceptional coolness and freshness in hot weather.

Little Black Dress (LBD): is an evening or cocktail dress, cut simply and often quite short. It is considered a staple in a woman's evening wardrobe.

Loafers: are also referred to as slip-ons and are typically low, lace-less shoes. The style usually has a moccasin construction with or without flaps or tassels.

Lycra Spandex: is a synthetic fiber known for its exceptional elasticity. It is strong, but less durable than natural Latex. It is a copolymer invented in 1959 by chemists C. L. Sandquist and Joseph Shivers at DuPont's Laboratory in Virginia. LYCRA is the brand name for spandex made by INVISTA formerly part of DuPont.

Madras: is a lightweight cotton fabric with patterned texture and plaid design, used primarily for summer clothing—pants, shorts, dresses and jackets. The fabric takes its name from the former English name of the city of Chennai, India. As a fabric, it is notable because the front and back of the fabric are indistinguishable.

Man Bags: are an alternative to backpacks and are common in Europe as a vehicle to carry one's wallet and keys for men; also known as a male purse or man-purse.

Mock Turtleneck: resembles the turtleneck with the soft fold at its top and the way it stands up around the neck, but both ends of the tube forming the collar are sewn to the neckline.

Novelty Fabrics: are fabrics that are novel striking, original or unusual.

Oxford cloth: is a woven fabric of a basket weave structure that is popular in men's dress shirts. Varieties in the cloth are the plain Oxford, the pinpoint Oxford and the more formal, royal Oxford.

Oxford shoe: is a style of laced shoe characterized by shoelace eyelet tabs that are stitched underneath the vamp, a construction method that is also referred to as "closed lacing". Oxfords originally came from the United Kingdom, where they were called **Balmorals** after the Queen's castle in Scotland, Balmoral

Parisian Knot: is a style of knot for scarves worn by men and women. To tie a Parisian knot take the scarf in both hands and fold it over lengthwise; drape it around your neck; insert the loose ends through the loop hanging in front of you and pull them through.

Patch pocket: is a bag, purse or pouch from fabric that is attached to the garment.

Pencil Skirt: is a slim-fitting skirt with a straight, narrow cut. Generally the hem falls to, or just below, the knee and is tailored for a close fit. It is named for its shape: long and slim like a pencil.

Pinking: is the result of using pinking shears for finishing edges of unfinished cloth. The sawtooth pattern does not prevent fraying but limits the length of the frayed thread thus minimizing damage.

Pocket Square: is a handkerchief that is used as a purely decorative accessory in a suit pocket.

Polo shirt: also known as a golf shirt or a tennis shirt, is a T-shaped shirt with a collar, typically a two- or three-button placket, and an optional pocket. Polo shirts are usually made of knitted cloth such as pique or jersey in cotton.

Polyester: is a category of polymers which contain the ester functional group in their main chain. Although there are many polyesters, the term "polyester" as a specific material commonly refers to polyethylene terephthalate (PET).

Princess Seams: create shape in dresses without darts by joining edges of different curvature. The resulting "princess seams" typically run vertically from the shoulder (or under the arm) over the bust point and down to the lower hem. This creates a long, slimming look, often seen in dresses with an "A-line" silhouette.

Raglan sleeve: is a sleeve that extends to the neckline. As opposed to the set in sleeve, the raglan allows for easier sizing and fit varieties.

Ratio: is the relationship in quantity, amount, or size between two or more things.

Raw silk: also known as Silk Noil, is a textured fabric with nubs and random flecks that can be dyed easily.

Regimental Stripe: is a pattern of British origin that is found commonly in ties with two or more colors alternating in a diagonal strip across the tie.

Ruffle shirt: is a fabric shape that can be either asymmetrical or not that is usually placed down the front placket of a shirt or around the collar. The ruffle introduces curved shapes into a somewhat tailored design.

Satin: is a weave that typically has a glossy surface and a dull back. It is a warp-dominated weaving technique that forms a minimum number of interlacings in a fabric. The fabric is formed with a satin weave using filament fibers such as silk, nylon, or polyester.

Scotch Plaid: is another name for a Tartan Plaid, with a criss cross design originally from Scotland.

Set-in sleeve: is a sleeve sewn into an armhole commonly found in suit jackets.

Sheath: is a type of dress designed to tightly fit the body. It is often made of a very light and thin material like cotton or silk and typically falls around the knees or lower thighs, and can be either strapped or strapless.

Shift or Chemise: refers to a short, sleeveless dress that hangs straight from the shoulders and fits loosely at the waist.

Silhouette: represents the outline of a shape and in fashion is used to describe the shape created by wearing clothing of a particular style.

Single Knit Jersey: refers to a single needle bed knitting the fabric. Fabric knitted on only one needle bed is jersey fabric. Jersey is considered to be an excellent fabric for draped garments, such as dresses and women's tops. An example of a single jersey knit is a T-shirt.

Skimmers: is a flat shoe with little or no heel in leather, suede or cloth that slips on. They are also referred to as ballet slippers or flats.

Split Skirt: were introduced during the Victorian Era (mid- to late-nineteenth century) so that women could sit astride a man's saddle rather than riding side-saddle. Culottes or split skirts were developed as an alternative to pants to provide women more freedom to do activities such as gardening, cleaning, bike riding, etc. and still look like they were wearing a skirt.

Spread Collars: measure from around 3½ to 6 inches between the collar points with the wider collars often referred to as *cutaway* or *Windsor* collars after the Duke of Windsor. This style of collar is considered formal.

Sport Coat or Sports Jacket: is a tailored jacket for men. Though it is of a similar cut and length to a suit jacket there are many differences. First, it is less formal and designed to be worn on its own rather than part of a suit. Styles, fabrics, colors and patterns are also more varied for sport coats with sturdier, thicker fabrics most often used, such as herringbone and tweed.

Sportswear: was originally clothing worn for sport or physical exercise and included footwear. Sportswear now refers to casual clothing worn for work or play.

Straight Leg: describes the shape of a pant leg. The leg is larger than those found in skinny jeans with a larger opening at the calf and ankle.

Suit Separates: are suit pieces such as jackets, pants, and skirts that can be purchased separately to add to one's wardrobe.

Tab collar: are pointed collars with two strips of fabric extending from the middle of the collar and joined behind the tie. These lift the tie, giving an arc effect similar to a pinned collar. The tabs can be closed with a metal snap, button or stud.

Tailor notched collar: is a wing-shaped collar with a triangular notch in it and often seen in blazers and blouses with business suits.

Tailored separates: include trousers, jackets and tops for women that can be coordinated and worn in place of a suit.

Tartan Plaid: is a pattern consisting of criss-crossed horizontal and vertical bands in multiple colors. Tartans originated in woven wool, but are now made in many other fabrics. Tartan was originally developed in Scotland as the foundation of the Scottish kilt.

Tencel: is the brand name for Lyocell, a regenerated cellulose fiber made from dissolving pulp (bleached wood pulp) more commonly known as rayon.

Terry Velour: is a plush, knitted fabric or textile. It is usually made from cotton but can also be made from synthetic materials such as polyester. Velour is used in a wide variety of applications, including clothing.

Topstitch: is a technique done usually with a sewing machine that is decorative in nature and found on necklines, hems and front closures to create a crisp edge and keep interfacings in place.

Tropical Weight Wool: is a two-ply, plain weave, worsted wool that is sturdy but lightweight, airy, and breathable. Tropical wool (sometimes called 'summer weight wool) is used in the production of warm-weather suits and other clothing items.

Tubular Silhouette: is a clothing article, more likely a dress, in the shape of a tube that is body hugging. The silhouette became popular in the 1950s.

Twill: is a type of textile weave that has a pattern of diagonal parallel ribs created by passing the weft thread over one or more warp threads and then under two or more warp threads and so on, with a "step" or offset between rows to create the characteristic diagonal pattern. This results in a fabric that drapes well and is sturdy. Examples include chino, drill, denim, gabardine, and tweed.

V- neckline: is formed by two diagonal lines from the shoulders that meet on the chest creating a V shape.

Welt pocket: is a small, flat pocket that is commonly used on the exterior and interior of a man's suit jacket or trouser. In women's wear welt pockets are used on blazers and suit jackets as well as pants. Depending on the design of the pants, the welt pocket may have a button closure.

Wingtips: are characterized by a pointed toe cap with extensions (wings) that run along both sides of the toe, terminating near the ball of the foot. Viewed from the top, this toe cap style is "W" shaped and looks similar to a bird with extended wings, explaining the style name that is commonly used in the United States. The toe cap is both perforated and serrated along its edges and includes additional decorative perforations in the center of the toe cap.

Wool: is the textile fiber obtained from sheep, goats, alpacas, rabbits, camels and other animals. The textile has several qualities that distinguish it from hair or fur: it is crimped, it is elastic, and it grows in clusters. The resulting fabric provides an insulating factor from the cold, wards off moisture and is breathable making it suitable for many climates.

Worsted Wool: is wool that has been manufactured in Worstead, England since the eighteenth century. Wool fibers are spun into compact, smoothly twisted yarn before weaving or knitting. The wool then goes through a second combing process which removes unwanted short fibers. Because the remaining long-staple fibers lay flat and parallel, worsted wool is a popular choice for suiting and dress trousers and is also wrinkle and crease resistant.

Selected Bibliography

Hall, Edward T. (1963). "Proxemics: A Study of Man's Spatial Relationship." *Man's Image in Medicine and Anthropology.* New York: International Press, 442-445.

Heslin, Richard cited in Knapp, Mark (1980), *Essentials of Nonverbal Communication*, New York: Holt, Rinehart and Winston, 152-155.

http://www.askmen.com

http://www.dropbox.com

http://www.edressme.com

http://www.greatestlook.com

http://ohioline.osu.edu/outside/stainrem.html

http://www.purseperfector.com

http://www.textileaffairs.com/lguide.htm

http://www.tsa.gov

Jackson, Carole (1984). *Color Me Beautiful*, New York: Holt, Rinehart and Winston.

Kaiser, Susan B. (1985). *The Social Psychology of Clothing and Personal Adornment*, New York: Macmillan Publishing Company.

Orgin and Franklin (2004), "Employee Dress Code Policies: Guidelines for Family Businesses" available at http://www.sbaer.uca.edu/research/usasbe/2004/pdf/24.pdf.

Seitz, Victoria A. (2000). *Your Executive Image*, Avon, Massachusetts: Adams Media.

Index

About the Author

Victoria Seitz, Ph.D. is an internationally recognized speaker, author, quoted expert and consultant with over 30 years experience in fashion and marketing. Clients of Dr. Seitz include Abbott Laboratories, General Dynamics, Northern Telecom, Texas Instruments, Yellow Freight Systems, Sally Beauty Company International, the United States Armed Forces, *Travellife* magazine, YWCA and Accountants Overload in addition to law firms, hotels, newspapers, universities, banks, credit unions, national and local community and professional organizations.

She is the author of four books including ***Your Executive Image*** (Adams Media) that has been translated into Chinese and ***Power Dressing*** (Ron Jon Publishing) and has appeared on TV and radio shows across the country and in Canada. She has been interviewed the world over on the topic of image and marketing and has been quoted in numerous publications including *Investor's Business Daily*, the *Los Angeles Times,* and *Business Week.* As well she has published hundreds of articles for newspapers, magazines, and various business journals on the topic of image and marketing. In addition, Dr. Seitz has made numerous presentations to groups throughout the world.

Dr. Seitz is listed in Who's Who in the South and Southwest, Who's Who Among Young Professionals of America, Who's Who of Emerging Leaders in America, Who's Who in Communications, the International Who's Who of Intellectuals, Dictionary of International Biography, Business Leaders of Tomorrow and Who's Who of Media. She was also voted one of the Outstanding Young Women of America, Who's Who of America's Best Teachers, Who's Who in Education, Who's Who in America, and Who's Who of American Women.

Dr. Seitz is currently a professor of marketing at California State University, San Bernardino. Prior to this she worked as an assistant designer for Frec Baggs, Inc., as a fashion coordinator for Burdines

Department Stores (Now Macy's), and in retail management for Saks Fifth Avenue. Dr. Seitz earned her Bachelor's degree at Kansas State University and Master's and Ph.D. in merchandising and marketing at Oklahoma State University.